SpringerBriefs in Economics

For further volumes:
http://www.springer.com/series/8876

Atanu Sengupta · Soumyendra Kishore Datta
Susanta Mondal

Productivity, Separability and Deprivation

A Study on Female Workers in the Indian Informal Service Sector

Springer

Atanu Sengupta
Soumyendra Kishore Datta
Susanta Mondal
Department of Economics
Burdwan University
Burdwan, West Bengal
India

ISSN 2191-5504 ISSN 2191-5512 (electronic)
ISBN 978-81-322-1055-9 ISBN 978-81-322-1056-6 (eBook)
DOI 10.1007/978-81-322-1056-6
Springer New Delhi Heidelberg New York Dordrecht London

Library of Congress Control Number: 2013933579

Printed on acid-free paper

Springer is part of Springer Science+Business Media (www.springer.com)

Preface

This book is a sequel to our joint efforts to unravel the gender gap in productivity and efficiency in service sector in India. Studies in this field in the Indian context are few and far between, although there exist ample studies in the context of secondary manufacturing sector. There are many cases in service sector where the final outcome is based on joint efforts in component jobs of both males and females. In such cases productivity is only partially separable. However, there are certain cases where there exists gender segregation in labour market and accordingly gender-based productivity turns out to be fully separable. Our study attempts to incorporate both these cases in deriving the female labour participation curve. The result is startling. Contrary to the popular belief, there are many cases where females are found to be more productive than the males. However they are always underpaid. An explanation for this is sought in the institutional barriers that tend to lower female participation in the productive sphere. The marginal product is enhanced but remuneration per worker falls.

We are extremely thankful to Springer (India) Pvt. Limited for offering us the proposal to write the book on this topic. Special thanks are due to Sagarika Ghosh who kept constant contact with us during the process of writing this book and kept track of our efforts and reminded us of the urgency of finishing this work within a reasonable time frame.

Atanu Sengupta
Soumyendra Kishore Datta
Susanta Mondal

Contents

Abbreviations

AICTE	All India Council for Technical Education
AMC	Account Maintenance Code
C.V.	Coefficient of Variation
C-D	Cobb-Douglas
CES	Constant Elasticity of Substitution
CRS	Constant Return to Scale
CSS	Circular Systematic Sampling
DME	Directory Manufacturing Establishment
DV	Deolalikar and Vijverberg
EST	Establishment
FAX	Fixational Auto Xerox
FDI	Foreign Direct Investment
FSU	First Stage Unit
GDP	Gross Domestic Product
GFCS	Gross Fixed Capital Stock
GVA	Gross Value Added
GVAPW	Gross Value Added Per Worker
HSE	Health and Safety Executive
IIT	Indian Institute of Technology
ILO	International Labour Organisation
ISD	International Subscriber Dialling
ISI	Indian Statistical Institute
JS	Jacoby and Skoufias
KLEMS	Capital, Labour, Energy, Materials and Services
LR	Literacy Rate
MNC	Multinational Corporation
MP	Marginal Product
NDME	Non-Directory Manufacturing Establishment
NIC	National Industrial Classification
NOO	Nature of Operation
NSS	National Sample Survey
NSSO	National Sample Survey Organisation

OAE	Own Account Enterprise
OAME	Own Account Manufacturing Establishment
OBC	Other Backward Class
OECD	Organisation for Economic Co-operation and Development
OLS	Ordinary Least Square
PCO	Public Call Office
PPS	Proportional to Size
PSU	Public Sector Unit
R. K. Mission	Ram Krishna Mission
S.D.	Standard Deviation
SAP	Structural Adjustment Programme
SE	Status of Enterprise
SEWA	Self-Employed Women's Association
SGO	Social Group of Owner
SR	State Region
SRSWOR	Simple Random Sampling Without Replacement
SC	Schedule Caste
ST	Schedule Tribes
STD	Subscriber Trunk Dialling
TFP	Total Factor Productivity
TFPG	Total Factor Productivity Growth
TOC	Type of Ownership Code
UFS	Urban Frame Survey
UK	United Kingdom
UN	United Nations
UNDP	United Nations Development Programme
UNESCO	United Nations Educational, Scientific and Cultural Organisation
UP	Uttar Pradesh
USU	Ultimate Stage Unit
UT	Union Territories
VFAW	Value of Fixed Asset per Worker
WB	West Bengal
WHO	World Health Organisation
YMCA	Young Men's Christian Association

Figures

Tables

Chapter 1
Introduction

Gender discrimination is now an important field in the development studies. Economists, sociologists and other branches of social thinkers pondered upon the issues regarding female deprivation and its impact. In many societies, ancient or modern, women occupy a significant position. Neglect of this segment is tantamount to neglecting the half-sky. Lot of human potential is lost in the hubris of social discrimination. This loss is not only social and psychological but also economical.

Recently there had been published a number of papers that tried to incorporate the contribution of women within the broader economic framework of the society (World Development 1995, 2000; Abu-Ghaida and Klasen (2004), Morrioson and Jutting (2005), Schober and Winter-Ebner (2011), Chen et al. (2013)). These analyses reveal the importance of female participation in the overall macro set-up of an economy. Arguments and counterarguments converged to the point that women deprivation is an issue that cannot be neglected either in the macroeconomic policies or in the designation of human welfare. In a sense gendering economics has been one of the main contentions in the current economic discourse.

An important issue however is to identify female contribution from the available statistics at the macro and micro level. Of special interest is the debate on distinguishing female productivity from male productivity in the arena of productive activities. It is rarely the case that detailed decomposition of female work activities is available. In such a scenario the necessary information has to be culled down from the more aggregative statistics. The econometric technique developed in this study may help to clear out some of the ambiguities that might have blighted developments in this area.

The econometric methodology is essentially built on the concept of separability. Traditionally, we may have two extreme viewpoints. Under zero separability it may be argued that male and female labour is indistinguishable. Both consist of an exercise and hence outcome of human dexterity, skill and mental exhaustion. Under these circumstances they are additive and inseparable.

The other extreme case is perfect separability. The distinction between male and female labour is real. It is based either on 'natural' distinction and/or socially

A. Sengupta et al., *Productivity, Separability and Deprivation*,
SpringerBriefs in Economics, DOI: 10.1007/978-81-322-1056-6_1,

constructed parameters. Thus these two types of labours are distinct and must be treated as completely different types of labour inputs.

In reality however the situation lies within these two extremes. On the one hand there are certain dimensions where the two types of labours are really indistinguishable. This may include the general, mental and physical exhaustion, intelligence and other soft-skill etc. On the other hand there are certain areas of marked differences. For example women are seen to concentrate in some particular types of jobs. Even among the jobs the duties are segregated along the gender lines. There are certain duties which seem to have been demarcated only for females (for example nursing). This distinction is as real as the similarity. Hence neither the zero separability nor the perfect separability would be ideal. It is rather essential to consider the case of imperfect separability. Various econometric techniques have been developed keeping in view the degrees of separability.

References

Abu-Ghaida D, Klasen S (2004) The costs of missing the Millennium development goal on gender equity. World Dev 32(7):1075–1107

Chen Z, Ge Y, Lai H, Wan C (2013) Globalization and Gender wage inequality in China. World Dev 44:256–266

Morrisson C, Jütting, JP (2005) Women's discrimination in developing countries: A new data set for better policies. World Dev 33(7):1065-1081

Schober T, Winter-Ebmer R (2011) Gender wage inequality and economic growth: Is there really a puzzle? – A comment. World Dev 39(8):1476–1484

World Development (1995) vol 23, no 11. Elsevier, Amsterdam

World Development (2000) vol 28, no 7. Elsevier, Amsterdam

Chapter 2
Review on Gender Studies

It is now widely recognized that in economy-wide macro contextual analysis, there should be put emphasis on the links between the paid and unpaid sectors of the economy or between productive and reproductive activities. Traditional macro-economic analysis has largely been silent about the segmentation of market in terms of gender, distinction between market paid labour and domestic unpaid labour and time allocation by women in productive sphere, reproductive purpose and other household activities. The introduction of structural adjustment policies has often intensified and made more obvious the nature of these links. There is however no unanimous view about its impact on gendered status of wellbeing of individuals. It might have increasing importance in the sphere of women's income-earning activities as male earnings decline, intensification of domestic work as household budgets shrink, or there may be instances of difficulties encountered by women in terms of access to markets. Thus it is held that macro models that consider technological change stimulated by structural adjustment should not be neutral with respect to gender.

Elson (1995) vehemently criticizes the macroeconomic models underlying the structural adjustment programs (SAP) for not being gender sensitive. The processes set in motion by SAPs are likely to have strong repercussions on the structure of entitlements to individuals in terms of their respective gender. She focuses on the necessity of identifying missing variables which may be categorized according to gender dimensions and argues for their inclusion in the macro models. She also puts stress on the issue of conceptualizing the economy as a gendered structure. This is tantamount to the view of considering the matrix of gender relations as an intervening variable in all economic activities. It is also stated that economic institutions which are not themselves intrinsically gendered, are nevertheless carriers of gender-laden culture and this has semblance to the views expressed by Whitehead (1979) and Elson (1993). It concludes that besides being inattentive to gender, these models also suffer from lack of incorporating concern for wastage of resources and economic deprivations arising from insufficient aggregate demand, undemocratic decision making and directly unproductive

A. Sengupta et al., *Productivity, Separability and Deprivation*,
SpringerBriefs in Economics, DOI: 10.1007/978-81-322-1056-6_2,

expenditures that support male power. This waste is, however, likely to be diminished by moves to more egalitarian systems of gender relations, entailing changes in the structure of entitlements and the social matrix in which macroeconomic processes are embedded.

According to Beneria (1995) feminist analysis has in recent years found an identity in the arena of economics. The influence of postmodernism and the development of feminist theory have together founded the base for the formation of the structure of economic theory and policy sensitive to gender issues. At the same time, feminist analysis has shifted from its main concentration on microeconomics to the discussion of macroeconomics. Emphasis is put on two areas in which progress toward engendering economic analysis has been made since the late 1970s: (a) the visibility of women's work and its inclusion in labor force and national accounting statistics, and (b) macroeconomic issues, with focus on the area of gender and development and of structural adjustment policies, with particular reference to alternative models to the orthodox structural adjustment packages.

Collier (1990) focused on "gender aspects of labour allocation during structural adjustment". The aspect of gender according to him, introduces some sort of issues on the basis of which data can be segregated and disaggregated. First, in case of employment and earning wages/income, women often face different constraints from men. But since with the advent of structural adjustment the constraints might be changing, it is imperative that separate studies be made across two genders rather than focusing on gender-undifferentiated averages. Second, as females and males have different tastes and preferences as well as propensities to consume particular public services, allocation of resources towards such gender sensitive public goods can have gender-differentiated impacts.

However treating gender simply as a form of disaggregation of agents, the aspect of gender inequality may not get adequate attention. It is embedded in social norms and cultural taboos and so the issue of women's discriminatory treatment in economic entitlements loses the centrality stress to the analysis. Hence Collier's analysis identifies the following four constraints that set in process a challenging role to women in deciding how to allocate their labor (a) discrimination against women outside the household; (b) copying of gender-specific role models; (c) asymmetric rights and obligations within households leading to weak incentives for women to undertake tasks in male-controlled production; (d) the burden of (biological) reproduction, leading to confinement to a restricted range of economic activities that are more easily compatible with motherhood.

Collier puts particular stress on barriers to women shifting to export crop production in sub-Saharan Africa. In this context, it is argued that constraints (b) and (c) are likely to be important. Gender specific role model imitation [constraint (b)] is held to be a factor constraining the adoption of export crops by female-headed households in situations where export crops have typically been grown under male control and are identified as 'male' crops. Further female heads of households often refrain from adopting export crops to the same degree as males owing to some undocumented differences between themselves and male heads of households (felt in the form of greater risk aversion because of greater direct responsibilities for well-being of children). Apart from this, marketing boards may operate out-grower schemes in ways that exclude many women farmers from obtaining licenses to grow specific tree crops. Another constraint emphasized by Collier in this context is constraint (c) i.e., asymmetric rights and obligations within households which provide weak incentive to women in male-headed households in allocating more time and effort in the sphere of export crop production.

Traditional development economists and modernization theorists usually hold the view that there is a correlative move between economic growth and women's incorporation to the labor force. But this idea was challenged by Boserup (1970) according to whom women become 'marginalized' during the process of economic development. She pointed out that men's privileged access to new technologies and education leads to growing productivity differences between men and women, and hence a decline in women's share of the labor force.

It is now widely recognized that since initiation of the process of structural adjustment and concomitant event of trade liberalization, there has been an untoward impact on the lives of the female folk in many developing economies. There had been a number of researches by non-mainstream economists which run counter to the view posed by mainstream economists who uphold the reduced impact on gender discrimination and increased female employment possibilities associated with macro adjustment policies. For instance Black and Brainerd (1999) advocate that increased openness to the world economy tends to reduce all kinds of discriminatory labor market practices, including those based on gender. Wood (1991) observed that trade between developed and developing countries corresponded with an increased female intensity of employment in developing countries and had no noticeable negative effect on the female intensity of employment in the traded-goods sector of industrialized countries. Recent findings by many cater to the view that gender inequalities in pay and working conditions generally have remained persistent in the face of increased female participation in paid employment following trade liberalization in developing countries.

In an attempt to undo the errors committed in the form of delinking gender dimensions in analyzing macroeconomic perspectives of liberalization programmes, feminist economists and international institutions such as the United Nations Development Programme (UNDP) and the World Bank, have included gender dimensions to analyse the consequences of global economic integration. Interest in studying gendered impacts of international trade have usually been through analyzing price, income and employment effects. Most of the empirical studies however have, due to easy availability of data, concentrated on the employment effects of trade.

There has been evidence from cross-country analysis that export promotion and trade liberalization policies have led to the feminization of the labor force in developing countries (Wood 1991; Cagatay and Ozler 1995). This finds support in a large number of country case studies which associate feminization of the labor force in developing countries with the spread of export led industrialization (Cagatay and Berik 1991). However, there is variation in the processes that have led to feminization of the labor force. In some cases feminization is a consequence of the shift of production to sectors where women have been traditionally employed (Wood 1991, 1994); in others feminization is the consequence of substitution of 'cheap' women labor for that of men (Standing 1989, 1999), while in some cases (Elson 1996) it is attributed to decline of jobs performed by men. These variations in interpretation of the process of feminization make it imperative that, cross-country studies be complemented by country-specific studies, and industry-level evidence complemented by plant-level evidence.

Using plant level data, Ozler (2000) focused on the relationship between export orientation and female share of employment in the Turkish manufacturing sector during the period 1983–1985. It was observed that female share of employment in a plant increases with the export to total output ratio of its sector. Using a logit regression positive estimate of the corresponding coefficient suggested that the plants having high export share in output were most likely to have female employees. Plants with high investment in machinery are less likely to have female employees as indicated with the negative and statistically significant parameter estimate. Again significant positive estimate of the coefficient, suggested that plants having few female employees were more likely to be small plants.

Trade liberalization has thus led to employment gains for women relative to men in Turkish manufacturing sector. At the same time women continue to be employed in low-skill and low pay jobs. Apart from this, in some subgroups in the sample, especially in plants having high proportion of female employment, and in large establishments, investment in machinery and equipment tends to reduce the female share. This finding provides support to arguments that employment gain of women following trade liberalization might be reversed as a consequence of improvement in technology.

Again based on import/export data across six European Union countries and developing countries, Schumacher (1984), find that there had been a distinct positive effect on male employment and negative effect on female employment. According to Baldwin (1984), women constitute a proportionately large share of workers displaced by foreign trade.

Focusing on the case of ten OECD countries, Kucera and Milberg (2000) identified gender bias in the employment effects associated with expansion of trade. Trade with developing countries revealed that in most cases a gender bias was present. North–South trade of manufactures has in many industrialized countries decreased female employment relatively more than male employment. In fact the issue largely depended on how a country's Textiles, Apparel, Leather and Leather Goods industry responded to foreign competition. The countries that ended up with the worst trade performance in these industries were those that experienced a sharp decline in female manufacturing employment as a whole. These results reconfirm the findings in the studies by Schumacher and Baldwin.

Analysis of cross country data pooled for 1985 and 1990, by Cagatay and Ozler (1995) reveal that the there is a U-shaped relationship between women's share of the labor force and the processes of long-term economic development. Controlling for the feminization U, it is also found by them that structural adjustment policies have led to an increase in feminization of the labor force via worsening income distribution and increased openness.

Seguino (2000) investigates empirically the impact of gender inequality in wages in export sector for a number of semi-industrialised export oriented economies on their economic growth. In these countries women provide the bulk of labor in the export sector and relatively lower wages for women workers leads to higher price elasticity of demand for exports from such countries. Empirical analysis of data covering the period 1975–1995, shows that GDP growth is positively related to gender wage inequality in contrast to recent work which suggests that income inequality slows growth.

Based on insights drawn from analysis related to gender based division in agrarian labour market in developing countries, Darity (1995) states that males have often been found interested in maximizing their income by undertaking production of an exportable cash crop by drawing women out of household/social maintenance activities, through coercive or compensatory actions. This introduces some sort of dichotomy.

The gender division of labor operates at two levels. First, women happen to be the sole workers in the social maintenance or 'subsistence' sector while males prefer to remain idle than to take part in household chores. Women's output in the household sector is a composite commodity that includes growing and preparation of food for their families, childrearing, and the upkeep of the home. Again despite working jointly in small holder export production, female and male jobs in this cash crop sector remain segmented and segregated. Work sphere of males are identified to be confined to land preparation while females engage in 'other tasks such as transplanting and weeding' which are usually identified as areas specific to womenfolk' (Elson 1991, p. 173). While there is no intrinsic difference in men's and women's abilities to perform one set of tasks or the other in the cash-crop sector, different efficiencies are associated with their efforts because the tasks are gender-typed.

According to Palmer (1995), conventional macroeconomic policy design has ignored the way in which gender relations result in distortions caused by biased and absent markets. Cutbacks in public expenditure have tended to worsen these distortions and crowd-out women's contributions to economic growth.

According to his observation, a great emphasis has been laid in many rural areas on voluminous production of export oriented primary products. This involves allocating extra effort towards attaining such objective through gender-typing of tasks that entails much more physical exertion on the part of female folk than their male counterparts. Apart from this, this has often been in addition to a more onerous burden of social reproduction work. Flourishing of revenue earnings through technological changes and a sound footing in international export market motivates male heads of households to exploit and dictate allocation of household resources, including women's labor. The coercive and exploitative treatment meted out to women in involving their participation for production of export cash crops, not only adds to the stress on women but may have untoward repercussion in the form of long term social costs manifest in stifled growth of the health and education of children. Palmer (1991) feels that any intensification of gender asymmetries of rights and access would worsen allocative inefficiency and raise long-term social costs. An important reason for these consequences lies in biased and absent markets; and the intensification of the distortions caused by market bias and market absence.

Gender bias in the labor market is extensive. Much of this emanates from segmentation and gender-typing of jobs. There has been a sharp growth in numbers of women undertaking causal or part-time, home-based work under contract (International Labor Office 1994). These women are generally young and poorly educated. But wage disparities cannot always be explained by the existence of different productivities or tasks. Women systematically receive lower wages than men because of lower socio-cultural values placed on women's work; and this means that women's labor is effectively subsidizing the return to other factors of production or the consumers of female labor-intensive products. Nor is this a small subsidy: women's wages tend to average only 66 % of men's. It is where markets are absent, however, that the greatest misallocation of women's resources occurs.

Howes and singh (1995) puts stress on a comparative gendered scenario of relative income and employment in the developed (North) and developing (South) countries arising out of long-term trends in the international economy. According to them, although there exists persistent gender division of labour, diverse forces operate in creating mass unemployment in the North with males affected differently compared to that of females. Although men's job growth rate has fallen as a sequel to deindustrialization, their rate of withdrawal from the labor force has hardly been commensurate with the rate of shrink of jobs. Further female entry into the labor force in feminized jobs occurred at a faster rate than they have been created. On the other hand, women in the south, have mostly chosen traditionally feminized jobs in the labor-intensive, export-oriented growing manufacturing sectors while in Latin America, entry has been largely in the service sector. Due to growing urbanisation and inflow of FDI, scope of male's absorption in traditional agricultural sector has been shrinking and that in domestic manufacturing has become relatively tardy. They suggests that attainment of an increase in the trend rate of growth in OECD countries and rise in world aggregate demand and production might constitute an optimal solution to the mass unemployment problem in the North, as well as in the South, and close the apparent competition for jobs across countries and across gender. However, such a trend rise in the long-term rate of growth of demand is conditioned by the emergence and functioning of new cooperative institutional arrangements within and between countries. Women should have an important and independent role in such a functional institutional set up.

Lim (2000) in her study analyzes the impact of East Asian crisis in the framework of business cycles and trade openness on the issue of relative employment prospect of males and females. During the second half of the 1980s there occurred a boost to male employment compared to that of females. However, as a sequel to East Asian crisis there was a big reversal to this phenomenon when there occurred a faster rate of growth of male unemployment than that of female unemployment (especially in urban areas). This happened despite a more rapid displacement of women workers from the manufacturing sector. The relative efficiency of female workers in service sector, resilience of the society to retain the services of females despite recessive tendencies, and flexibility of female employment in wholesale and trade sector during the crisis explains the relative female advantage in employment during the crisis. Increased female labor force participation and longer working hours for women relative to men during the crisis points to increased female employment and work hours in the labor market as a major coping mechanism during the crisis. However, the reason behind this increased labour hours for females may be attributed to lower female wage, weak workers union and flexibility of female employment and hence their demand in employment market during the crisis period. According to this chapter, the boom-bust cycles in the macro economy are not gender neutral and is reflective of disparate distribution of working hours and wages across males and females which mostly ill-serve the interests of female folk.

Floro and Dymski (2000) explored the gender dimensions of household borrowing and credit repayment in the context of financial crisis. This study seeks to bridge the gap caused by neglect of gender issues pertaining to financial crises by exploring a suggestive micro-foundational model of unequal gender power and cost-bearing in a borrower household. It addresses the question of what happens to gender relations within the household as an economy goes through financial liberalization and crisis. By drawing on East Asian experience, specifically that of middle-class households, focus is made on the processes of decision-making and risk bearing in the context of credit supported household production and decision making environment. The purpose is to identify some previously invisible gender aspects of financial liberalization and crisis by analyzing household borrowing, asset acquisition and liquidation and financial fragility at different stages of the financial cycle. The constructed model focuses on the variations in intra-household gender relations that are linked with vicissitudes in financial conditions and associated credit-market processes.

It is held that financial liberalization can increase employment status of women, and lead to an increased lending to households; enhanced access to financial capital can facilitate the growth of household enterprises which may have a palliative impact on women's reproductive labour by raising the stock of household assets and thus female empowerment. With strengthened financial transactions and expertise to handle related matters, women are likely to feel increased power in domestic decision making, and their risk-aversion decrease. However, the burden of time bound interest payment associated with adoption of credit based expenditures make households financially fragile; Females in the process are exposed to vulnerable position since their cash-flow dependence increases whereas their support networks erode. In times of financial crisis, women's economic and social status turns tenuous with gradual discriminatory treatment in terms of wages, reduction of women's earned income, loss of control over assets, and stifled voice in household decisions. As a result women are virtually coerced to feel the brunt of marginalized social status with no alternative than to bear a much skewed share of household adjustment costs.

Braunstein (2000) develops a structuralist macroeconomic model and combines it with a model of family structure for analyzing the issue of how gender relations affect multinational operations and considering how women's roles outside the formal market sector impact the profitability of multinational investment. It is argued that the extent to which women and men share the costs of social reproduction at the household level is a central determinant of women's labor supply and the profitability of investment.

One major focus has been made to specify the constraints imposed by capital mobility on the prospects for increased living standards and increased equality for women. Another important dimension of the analysis has been consideration of multinational investment through a gender sieve for providing significant insights into the behavior of MNCs and FDI. Such a focus is important for both developing and developed countries. MNC investment based strategy of development has been a significant factor in the economic development of a small but important group of countries in the last several decades.

In developing a model of family structure and female labour supply, it is emphasized that macroeconomists and development economists hardly paid adequate attention to the unique factors affecting female labor supply, overlooked how workers' productive roles are influenced by factors outside the factory door, and the institutional and social contexts in which they live, create fundamental differences between the labor supply behavior of women and men. Specifically, attention were not given to factors affecting the productivity of nonmarket work, including fertility and urbanization; institutional factors such as educational access, the public provision of childcare and enforcement of child support responsibilities and bargaining position and inequality in the household.

There may be complex interaction among these factors in influencing female labour supply. Fertility decline is often accompanied by an increase in women's labor force participation (Easterlin 1989); high incidences of male desertion and non-marital births probably lower women' reservation wages; increases in female education raise the reservation wage of young women who remain in school longer and change the composition of the female labor force. Women having little bargaining power in the family, may be barred from entering the labor market by husbands who feel afraid of the loss of their own bargaining power with gaining of financial autonomy on the part of their wives.

Theoretical framework suggests that gender relations can affect the profitability of investment via their impact on the female reservation wage. This work also suggests in what contexts female autonomy may be consistent with attracting and/or retaining multinational capital. The analysis concludes with exploring the impacts of three policies: (1) an increase in aggregate demand, (2) a decline in gender wage discrimination, and (3) an increase in women's productivity in the market, along with putting some general observations about the interaction between women's power in the family and the ability of countries to attract and retain multinational capital.

Erturk and Cagatay (1995) analyzes the macroeconomic implications of cyclical and secular movements in the feminization of the labor force and changes in the intensity of female household labor. In this context a simple Kaldorian model is used that makes output adjustment (i.e., changes in the rate of capacity utilization rate) a function of the gap between investment and savings. It is assumed that a rise in the feminization of the labor force stimulates investment while a rise in the intensity of female household labor raises savings. Feminization of the labor force is assumed to vary counter-cyclically and is therefore an inverse function of the capacity utilization rate. The analysis shows that for a gender-based recovery to succeed, the impact of feminization of the labor force on investment must be stronger than the impact a rising intensity of female household labor has on savings. The implications are that high and high middle income countries are more likely to benefit from feminization processes.

Erturk and Darity (2000) undertake a simple theoretical exercise that highlights the importance of gender relations in the standard analysis of trade liberalization and economic growth. Using a simple two differential-equation model and phase diagram technique, focus is made on the possible interaction between economic growth and changes in the gender composition of the labor force. It is assumed that gender relations on the growth trajectory differ across countries at different layers of development.

The analysis puts stress on two avenues through which gender relations can affect long term economic growth: (a) female labor within the household shoulders the social cost of reproducing the labor power in the economy sans any payment and (b) female labor outside the household performs the same work men do at comparatively lower payment. In the entire analysis, the economic impact of increasing feminization of the labor force works through these two linkages. In relation to the first, ceteris paribus, increasing female participation of the labor force has a negative effect on output. For the extent to which the cost of reproducing the labor power is subsidized by unpaid female labor is likely to diminish as women are drawn in large numbers into paid employment. In relation to the second, ceteris paribus, women's increasing labor force participation is likely to have a positive effect on output due to lower wage costs. The relative weight of these two gender impacts may diverge across countries at different levels of development.

On this basis it is observed that benefits from trade liberalization between the North and the South can be offset by changes in the female share of employment caused by a new global division of labor brought about by changing trade relations. The outcome of the analysis implies that gender relations possibly can put a stumbling block to the flow of economic benefits usually associated with trade liberalization process.

Grown et al. (2000) alludes to the fact that an inegalitarian gendered view is central to the report prepared by the UN Division for the Advancement of Women's Survey on the Role of Women in development (United Nations 1999). Based on a variety of country and plant level evidences it is stated that, gender inequality is persistent with feminization of the labour force. First it focuses on how trade liberalization affects women's share of paid employment, and second how it leads to transformation of the conditions of paid work, so that several jobs are turned casual, irregular, flexible and perilous, similar to characteristics typical in case of 'women's work'. This also has implications about how severe competition in international sphere affects caring work borne mostly by women. Based on a variety of country and plant level references it is stated that, although on an average, greater trade openness usually increases women's share of paid employment, it does not necessarily imply reduction in discrimination against employed women, nor does it necessarily reduce women's share of the unpaid work served through providing familial care. In some instances women have been displaced from employment by trade liberalization. In agriculture in developing countries, women have been ill-equipped, as compared to men, to shield themselves from negative effects and take advantage of positive effects of trade liberalization. This is because women have control over fewer assets than men. Persistence of vertical occupational segregation has also intensified, in the sense that women remained highly concentrated at the bottom of the job hierarchy, despite a substantial decline of 'horizontal' segregation (the distribution of men and women) across the globe.

Singh and Zammit (2000) state that while there has been a substantial attention to the gender dimensions of international trade, the gender aspect pertaining to international capital flows has been a relatively unexplored area. Some of the most important works have dealt with the relationship between exports, female employment and women's wages in developing countries. Two issues are stress on in this analysis: (a) how the long term rate of growth of GDP and its stability is influenced by freer private capital flows and (b) what the implications of these changes are for wages, employment and the unpaid labor of women.

From the perspective of macro dynamic sense, it is observed that females are loser than males from sluggish or unstable economic growth, financial crises and meltdowns, and this condition worsens during periods of intensified slump since women become exposed to great burden and risk of disempowerment through retrenchment in the absence of a strong social insurance and security. In order to avoid such situation prudent macroeconomic policies need to be pursued which foils the emergence of such unsustainable fiscal or balance of payments disequilibria. In this context it is suggested that women make an organized move and ventilate their aspirations and demands in a unified manner that may be in conformity with their interest and their views may be integrated into the inputs for evolving a new global financial order.

In the context of agricultural production in Africa, Warner and Campbell (2000) attempt to detect the elements of subordination or coercion in male–female relations. Citing the case of Tanzania, they identify ample evidences which indicate gender-based intra-household conflict over consumption and production decisions. Using Stackelberg type functions, this analysis contributes to the understanding of household responses based upon gender specific non-symmetric assumptions relating to allocative prerogatives within the household. On the basis of gender-sensitive analysis there is observed absolutely unequal labor allocation within the household. This has implications for unequal distribution of final consumption (men influencing final distribution to the benefit of their own allocative priorities) and women struggling within their constrained menu of choices. Typically this analysis focuses on the lack of female control over property and cash revenues generated from structural adjustment related policy oriented stress on increased production of cash crops. Although this framework of analysis is consistent with the usual assignment of female responsibility towards subsistence production, this does not confine them to jobs mutually exclusive to those males since often they are observed to engage in cash crop production. This finding is in line with the works of Bertell (1986) and Omari (1988) according to whom, despite right to production, women can hardly enjoy the right to control the use of their products as decision making power continue to be centred around the male members in all farming related operations.

It is well known that a great number of African countries suffer from most oppressive economic institutions manifest in the form of male-centered inheritance/control of land (Bernia 1982). For instance in Tanzania, although formal legal system approves of access to land by all people, women are disbanded by customary law from direct control of land and they have to depend on their husbands for allocating land to them (Ghai et al. 1979). The women are usually allowed allotment of certain pieces of land under the strenuous obligation to provide food for the rest of the family members. This results in certain amount of intra-household rent reallocation in which males enjoy and appropriate the fruits of labour offered by females in cash crop production, who also feel deprived in having equal access to credit market like that of their male counterparts.

All these writings are indicative and critical of either advertent or inadvertent omission of gender issues in traditional macroeconomic perspective of an economy's development process. The fact that there might be possible gender impacts with the unleashing of the structural adjustment programme, could not be properly visualized by the proponents of the programme through a circumspect view from macroeconomic dimensions. Several writers criticized this stoical view taken with regard to gender issues in traditional macro economic analysis.

It has been identified in the literature that although feminization of employment has happened in many countries due to SAP, this has happened mostly in traditional export oriented sector where the female folk have been subjugated to relatively lower payments compared to male counterparts, casualisation and insecured status of employment as well as often increased burden of unpaid household chores to balance between both domestic and market works. Further during periods of financial crisis, females have been victim of credit squeeze. Thus in the literature there are now ample references to the impact on gender dimensions as a sequel to adjustments in macroeconomic policies. The extant literature is however mute as to the quantification of productivity of female labour vis-à-vis male labour in own account enterprises (OAEs) and establishment.

In a recent paper Cuberes and Teignier (2011) examine the quantitative effects of gender gaps in entrepreneurship and labor force participation on aggregate income. A simple theoretical model is used to imply the negative impact of gender gaps on resource allocation and aggregate labor productivity. The model is then calibrated and simulated to study the quantitative impacts of gender inequality.

It is revealed from empirical data that the gender gap in entrepreneurs has significant effects on resource allocation and aggregate productivity. While the gap from formal employment does not affect productivity, there is found large impacts on per capita income. Specifically, if no women works as an entrepreneur, output per worker would drop by more than 10 %, while if the labor force participation of women be nil, income per capita would decrease by almost 40 %. However, there is no reference in the paper as to the productivity difference across gender and their respective payments.

In this perspective there is a novel dimension in the present work as it ventures into the hitherto unexplored/little attended task of isolating and quantifying gender–wise labour productivity and associating it with corresponding payments.

References

Baldwin R (1984) Trade policies in developed countries. In: Jones R, Kenen P (eds) Handbook of international economics, vol 1. Amsterdam, North-Holland

Beneria L (1995) Toward a greater integration of gender in economics. World Dev 23(11):1839–1850

Bernia L (1982) Women in development: the sexual division of labor in rural societies. Praeger, New York

Bertell T (1986) Effects of finnish development cooperation on Tanzanian women: in Tanzanian rural women and their crucial role in development. Institute of Development Studies, Helsinki

Black SE, Brainerd E (1999) Importing equality? The effects of increased competition on the gender wage gap, Staff report/74, Federal Reserve Bank of New York (pp 32) http://www.ny.frb.org/rmaghome/staff_rp/sr74.pdf

Boserup E (1970) Woman's role in economic development. St. Martin's Press, New York

Braunstein E (2000) Engendering foreign direct investment: family structure, labor markets and international capital mobility. World Dev 28(7):1157–1172

Cagatay N, Berik G (1991) Transition to export-led growth in Turkey: is there a feminization of employment? Capital and Class 43:153–177

Cagatay N, Ozler S (1995) Feminization of the labor force: the effects of long-term development and structural adjustment. World Dev 23(11):1883–1894

Collier P (1990) Gender aspects of labor allocation during structural adjustment, unpublished manuscript. Oxford: Oxford Unit for the Study of African Economics, Oxford University

Cuberes D, Teignier M (2011) Gender Inequality and Economic Growth. Background paper for the world development report 2012: gender equality and development

Darity W (1995) The formal structure of a gender-segregated low-income economy. World Dev 23(11):1963–1968

Easterlin R (1989) Fertility. In: Eatwell J, Milgate M, Newman P (eds) Social economics. Macmillan, New York

Elson D (1991) Male bias in macroeconomics: the case of structural adjustment. In: Elson D (ed) Mule bias in the development process. Manchester University Press, Manchester, pp 164–190

Elson D (1993) Gender-aware analysis and development economics. J Int Dev 5(2):237–247

Elson D (1995) Gender awareness in modeling structural adjustment. World Dev 23(11):1851–1868

Elson D (1996) Appraising recent developments in the world market for nimble fingers. In: Chhachhi A, Pittin R (eds) Confronting state, capital and patriarchy: women organizing in the process of industrialization. Macmillan, Basingstoke

Erturk K, Cagatay N (1995) Macroeconomic consequences of cyclical and secular changes in feminization: an experiment at gendered macro modeling. World Dev 23(11):1969–1977
Erturk K, Darity W (2000) Secular changes in the gender composition of employment and growth dynamics in the north and the south. World Dev 28(7):1231–1238
Floro M, Dymski G (2000) Financial crisis, gender, and power: an analytical framework. World Dev 28(7):1269–1283
Ghai D, Lee MJ, Radwan S (1979) Overcoming rural development. Paper prepared for a workshop on alternative agrarian systems and rural development, Arusha, Tanzania, 4–14 April
Grown C, Elson D, Cagatay N (2000) Introduction. World Dev 28(7):1145–1156
Howes C, Singh A (1995) Long-term trends in the world economy: the gender dimension. World Dev 23(11):1895–1911
International Labor Office (1994): Summary of the discussion. International Forum on: Equality for women in the world of work: challenges for the future, International Labor Office, Geneva. l–3 June
Kucera D, Milberg W (2000) Gender segregation and gender bias in manufacturing trade expansion: revisiting the 'wood asymmetry'. World Dev 28(7):1191–1210
Lim JY (2000) The effects of the East Asian crisis on the employment of women and men: the Philippine case. World Dev 28(7):1285–1306
Omari CK (1988) Rural women, informal sector and household economy in Tanzania. WIDER working papers 79, World Institute for Development Economics Research
Ozler S (2000) Export orientation and female share of employment: evidence from turkey. World Dev 28(7):1239–1248
Palmer I (1991) Gender and population in the adjustment of African economies: planning for change. International Labor Office, Geneva
Palmer I (1995) Public finance from a gender perspective. World Dev 23(11):1981–1986
Schumacher D (1984) North-South trade and shifts in employment. Int Labour Rev 123(3):333–348
Seguino A (2000) Gender inequality and economic growth: a cross-country analysis. World Dev 28(7):1211–1230
Singh A, Zammit A (2000) International capital flows: identifying the gender dimension. World Dev 28(7):1249–1268
Standing G (1989) Global feminization through flexible labor. World Dev 17(7):1077–1096
Standing G (1999) Global feminization through flexible labor: a theme revisited. World Dev 27(3):583–602
United Nations (1999) World survey on the role of women in development: globalization, gender, and work. United Nations, New York
Warner JM, Campbell DA (2000) Supply response in an agrarian economy with non-symmetric gender relations. World Dev 28(7):1327–1340
Whitehead A (1979) Some preliminary notes on the subordination of women. IDS Bulletin 37(4):24–27
Wood A (1991) North-South trade and female labour in manufacturing: an asymmetry. J Dev Stud 27(2):168–189
Wood A (1994) North-South trade employment and inequality: changing fortunes in a skill-driven world. Clarendon Press, Oxford

Chapter 3
Case Studies: Implication of Separability

The pivotal point in our study is the concept of separability of labour. In the traditional economics gender differences in labour use is rarely made. The qualities of male and female labour are treated perfectly homogeneous (and also additive). This standpoint, we can regard as zero separability. The other extreme is where male and female labours are treated non-substitutable and non-additive. In fact, they may be treated as two different types of labour inputs. This is what we can call as perfect separability. However these are two extreme cases and the reality lie in between. While there are certain issues where there is almost no difference between male and female labour, there are cases where the distinction is relevant and perceptible. Such differences might be attributed to social construction or 'natural divisions'. However the fact is that the distinction remains. For example, in primary education male and female are perfectly substitutes. In fact some sociologists claim that the females are more suitable for these jobs. However as we move up the ladder of education, the proportion of females drastically falls. The issue of separability is crucial in this context. In this chapter we provide certain case studies in this regard.

3.1 Labour Separability: Gender Dimension

One of the perplexing issues in social science is the issue of gender dimension in the labour process (DN and GK 1989). In the traditional literature the division of labour between genders is assumed to be 'natural'. Men are generally prescribed for jobs that require more physical strains while the 'less' strenuous job is allocated for the females. In the economic literature this view is persuaded by several authors (Becker 1975, 1985; Boserup 1970).

Theoretically a number of issues emanate here. Classicists believed that wage differential exists due to difference in level of skill. According to Cairnes (1874) men and women can never be substituted for one another on the same job

A. Sengupta et al., *Productivity, Separability and Deprivation*,
SpringerBriefs in Economics, DOI: 10.1007/978-81-322-1056-6_3,

and so wage differential is acceptable and justifiable. Webb and Webb (1897) showed that men and women could play mutually complementary roles in productivity, especially in industries. Thurrow (1969) opined that discrimination may be manifest in the form of pre–market discrimination in which women find restricted entry into the labor market and post market discrimination in which females with productivity at par with males receive lower wages for the same kind of job. According to Bergman's (1974) overcrowding model, however, employers' taste for discrimination against women results in the segregation of two sets of occupations for males and females leading to difference in their job opportunities. These opportunities may be low in female–dominated occupations in relation to their supply. This kind of discrimination results in both wage and productivity differential between potentially equal productive males and females. According to human capital theorists like Becker, Schultz, Polachek etc., an individual could make in investment in himself by devoting time for education, acquiring skill and work experience. Larger investment is likely to draw higher returns. They hold the view that females in general abstain from participating in those occupations that require substantial experience and prolonged period of training. According to them women cannot be treated as perfect substitutes for men. Hence it is not unbecoming that male–female productivity and wage differential might exist when women accumulate less human capital through work experience due to their relatively short stay in labor market compared to male counterparts.

It is also argued that male–female productivity differential may be due to a combination of varying degree of work effort as well as mental and physical capabilities. Pioneering work has been done by Gunderson (1975, 1989). Oaxaca (1973) was first to decompose the male female premium into two parts: one that is explained by economic characteristics and the other being a residual. This residual is alleged to be an indicator of gender discrimination (Blau et al. 1998). On the other hand a group of writers attribute this to the inherent differences in characteristics among men and women (Wise 1975; Duncan 1976; Becker 1985; Long 1995; Hakim 2000; Paarsch and Shearer 2004). These differences may be manifested in mental and physical attributes (such as motivation, aggressiveness, ability to conduct strenuous physical jobs, family attachment etc.) as well as preference to certain types of jobs.

It is argued that male is more suitable for works that requires considerable amount of physical effort than their female counterparts. On the other hand, woman has to bear the burden of household chores (such as baby rearing, cooking, cleansing etc.). In fact Becker (1985) has suggested that women have a comparative advantage in high effort domestic tasks which may cause them to supply less effort in the labor market than men. This tends to depress their work effort. With increasing commercialization and expansion of market however market valuation of women's work may increase. Hence they may be motivated by better earning possibilities that were non-existent previously. In this context it can be said that increased market opportunities could improve female productivity and participation.

However, recently a number of social scientists have begun questioning the so called 'natural' division (Rosaldo 1974; Chodorow 1974; Murdock 1968; Coontz and Henderson 1986; Mukhopadhyay and Higgins 1988; DN and GK 1989).[1] These anthropologists and social scientists argued that even in the primitive society women do take part in all types of economic activities, including hunting and gathering.

For example Mukhopadhyay and Higgins (1988) note that among the Agta tribes of Phillippines women regularly go to hunting. They argue that Akta women of every age group including pregnant, menstruating and lactating females do go to hunting. They kill the same range of animals, including large animals and working in mixed-sex and/or the same-sex team. The Akta women believe that hunting is not incompatible with child rearing activities. Even carrying babies on hunting trips is not a hindrance. The only hindrance is the lack of hunting dogs.

A study by Sen (1966) on the foraging tribes in Jharkhand reveals almost the same features. Among the Birhor tribes, hunting of small game by the women is a regular activity. The rituals 'Jani Shikar' (women's hunt) is found among the Oraon, Munda, Santal and Ho tribes of Jharkhand.

Among the agricultural tribes of Jharkhand, Rosaldo (1974) found the demarcation between public and private domains. Women are not allowed to perform in the public domain though they perform in the private domain. There is a very strong taboo against women ploughing or even touching plough, and against women roofing the hut. However there are strong indications that these activities were done by females in the earlier period. But among the Birhors and Korwas no such provision was available.

Given the inconclusive debate we feel that the gender division of labour is both a result of social taboo and/or by any 'natural' forces. Being deprived of rich set of activities, women get huddled into their own nest. These have wide implication for the issue of full and partial separability. Thus depending on circumstances the discrimination in the labour process emanates either as full or partial separability.

We now turn to certain micro case studies in the available literature to further our point. These studies will reveal the nature of separability and its consequences in the overall production process.

3.2 Male–Female Separability: Primary and Secondary Sector

A case of separability between sex compositions of labour in the agricultural sector has been pointed out by a number of authors. These cases are found in galore in underdeveloped economies though the anthropologists argue the distinction is more an outcome of a social construct than of any real difference. However,

[1] We give only a few references of the first literature that questioned this naturalized division.

studies in India, Malaysia and in other underdeveloped areas repeatedly reveal separability of duties between male and female workers. Among all the studies, we bring in the important work by Deolalikar and Vijverberg (1987).

Deolalikar and Vijverberg (1987) applied the homogeneity test between hired and own labour in agriculture. They used the firm level data of India and Malaysia. Their analysis reveals that there exist substantial differences between family and hired labour in India and Malaysia. They tried to unravel this mystery by using the limited data set they had at their hand.

One of their interesting conjectures is that the difference between hired and own labour might be a reflection of the gender difference between those two categories of labour. Unfortunately the Indian data do not reveal much difference between the family and hired labour. In the case of Malaysia however, female works mostly as family workers. However it may be imprudent to draw any firm conclusion about the gender divide of tasks from this simple analysis. As Deolalikar and Vijverberg (1987) note, there are seasonality and specificity in the labour use. In the slack season the work of transplantation, seedling cares are done. Women are specialized for some of these jobs. Similarly in the peak season, harvesting and threading are done. Here again some tasks are specific to women.

Parr (1988) has beautifully explained how gender division of labour took place in the hosiery industry in two different regions: English east midlands and in southwestern Ontario in Canada. At the beginning of the century English hosiery industry was a mixed gendered occupation. Seamers were predominantly females from the domestic sphere while the fixers with mechanical aptitude were uniformly male. Within 50 years two changes occurred in hosiery industry: human labour being replaced by steam power and production mode changed from workshop to factory production. With this, the sexual division of labour in this industry was reformulated within those two regions. But the ways in which this gender division occurred within two regions differed markedly. In the first region managers preferred males over females and in the second case, the structure of hosiery industry in Ontario favoured females over males.

In the east Midlands, from the traditions of workshops there were women knitters side by side the male. In the domestic production sphere there was flexibility in gender division because the number of available male and females at a given time in a family was fixed. Men often knit while women seamed and the struggling stockinger was usually male. But in the mid-nineteenth century circular machine was introduced which was well adapted for domestic use and was women friendly. By the 1890s a divided interest entered the trade. Men began to believe that status of male knitters has been devalued because of their heavy dependence on women's circular machines. So they began to claim that all knitters were historically and preferably male. As a consequence of this movement, the seaming and fixing jobs were not reassigned between men and women, but the gender of knitters was contested. Hosiery firms employed surplus local female labourers as knitters, seamers and menders and male in overseeing and fixing activities. When job was not available locally for male, hosiery manufacturers assigned all knitting jobs to male fearing the loss of female labour if families were not retained in the district. In this way male capitalists conceded the male unionists' claim that men should be the knitters locally.

Subsequently the hosiery unions took an active role in the reformulation of gender divisions in knitting, safeguarding the interests of men to the detriment of female members. Union leaders did not give much attention to the benefit plans or interventions on behalf of women. Still in the 1930s unions were "run by the men for the men". Female labourers were not permitted to work on machines ordinarily handled by men, but men's claim to circular machines was treated sympathetically.

Besides, both manufacturers and male workers believed that gender-specific restrictions on women's night work were appropriate. Male workers demanded overtime in rush seasons which maximized their earnings and emphasised their preference over female knitters—whose home responsibility conflicted with extended hours. Eventually most knitting became male dominated activities. It is only after World War II, that the gender balance had been re-established in midlands factory knitting rooms as a result of radical changes in the technology, labour process and relations between owners and workers.

There were certain differences between East midlands and Southwest Ontario in the structure of firms, the pattern of labour recruitment and the strength of workers' organization. Whereas midlands industry was characterised by many small independent firms, specializing in one phase of the production process, the Ontario industry was oligopolistic and vertically integrated.

Like Midlands, Ontario knitting industry also employed a large number of female labour. Seaming activities, which was labour intensive was dominated by female workers. Ontario Managers applied the strategy of mixing men's and women's job to secure a stable female labour force. They had more flexibility in achieving this goal due to the diversified structure of Canadian firms. They created some separate departments like spinning, dying, pressing and box-making particularly for female in order to assure labour segmentation that kept its seaming and finishing departments safely separate for females, carrying low wages. These jobs were previously dominated by men alone. When demand for women mill workers had exceeded the supply of nearby farmer's daughters, they began to recruit overseas. They brought large number of young women from midlands on contract labour scheme. They also used gender-specific recruitment overseas to secure extra women employees for boom times. This necessitated reassigning some jobs to male workers which were previously held by either men or women.

Unlike Midlands, Ontario managers were least influenced by unions, so far as shifting work is concerned. They drew the dividing line between men's and women's work in knitting rooms across day and night. This gender division between day and night work was done based on the social belief that male knitters controlled the machines, while female knitters only cared for them. Boys and girls worked in day shift with adult female knitters and adult males worked in night shift. The best male knitters earned 20 % more than the best female knitters, but they worked longer hours. But soon the male workers realized the physical strains caused by sleepless nights. But as the alternative job opportunities were limited, they were compelled to adjust with longer hours of work at night with same rate as women were assigned by day.

On the basis of their experience immigrant women workers preferred Ontario while men thought the midlands a better place to work. As a result several households of Canada were divided after a few years: men returning to their home country and women remained in the overseas with their children. This sexual division and gender hierarchies in knitting industry favoured women in Ontario and men in the organised work-places of midland.

One of the most prevalent cases of gender discrimination in the labour process may be visualised in the construction industry. According to the official statistics (Barnabas et al. 2009) 50 % of the workforce in the construction industry is women. Historian Habib (2008) noted that even in the mediaeval India women were regularly employed for carrying the constructible materials in the construction site. He has provided a mediaeval picture to support his claim. This clearly indicates that this activity was designated for women, ever since the mediaeval time. Even today carrying activities are mostly shifted to women. They are traditionally referred to as 'Jogandar'. It is ironical that this activity requires a huge amount of strenuous physical labour which is generally assumed to be unbecoming of a woman. This type of occupational segregation is found both in developed and in developing countries, with women concentrated in low-paid jobs and men undertaking the better-paid skilled work (Baruah 2010). It occurs mainly due to lack of appropriate training, inadequate occupational information, multiple roles of women and above all employers' attitude towards women employees, etc. (Vaid 1999). This is a typical case of duty separability within the labour process. However such duty separability does not transform itself into full labour separability. The reason is simply because construction work is a coherent activity that requires combined effort of male and female workers. Hence it is difficult to disentangle their contribution in the final output (Picture 3.1a, b).

Barnabas et al. (2009) conducted a survey on the construction workers in Tiruchirapalli district in Tamilnadu. They found that about half of the workforce in the construction industry is women. Initially, women join as unskilled workers and remain unskilled throughout their working life span. But men get proper training to upgrade their construction skills to get promoted as masons, supervisors and contractors. They find that there is an inherent gender bias against women.

Picture 3.1a Women workers in the construction site

Picture 3.1b Women workers in the construction site

There is also a general belief that women workers cannot be trained as men in the construction sector, even though the women have the necessary skill, capability and desire to become mason. Even though the contractors are willing to give them training and placement in the construction sector as masons and other skilled works, the social forces prevents them to remain in the unskilled inferior works.

Another study conducted by SEWA Academy (1999)[2] in Ahmedabad city finds that most of the women workers (92 %) in the construction sector are unskilled workers, engaged in the work of carrying loads of cement, bricks, concrete etc. and a very few of them are engaged in the semi-skilled work like plastering and concrete mixing. In contrast, only 38 % of men workers are engaged in load carrying and the remaining portion constitute providers of semi-skilled or skilled work like masonry, tile laying, centering etc. There were also considerable earning differences between male and female workers reflecting their skill differences.[3]

While the demand for skilled construction workers is increasing rapidly, that for unskilled labour is dwindling. This is specially true in the urban areas, with its significantly higher demand bias for skilled over unskilled labour. In such a situation, unskilled workers in general and women in particular will gradually be eliminated from the construction industry (Baruah 2010).

3.3 Male–Female Separability: Tertiary Sector

Another area of low-skilled women employment happens to be the hotel and restaurant activity. In this sector the women typically perform the activity of washing and cleaning the utensils. They are allotted the duties of cutting vegetables, pasting

[2] Source: Barnabas et al. (2009).

[3] The average earnings of women were Rs. 60 per day as against Rs. 128 for men.

Picture 3.2 Women worker washing utensils in a private roadside hotel

of spices etc. that may be deemed as secondary cooking activity. These activities are essential for the cooking. However the primary cooking activity is done by a male cook or his associates. Again there is a duty division that is difficult to identify as labour separability. This is because the primary and secondary activities are complement to each other. It is again difficult for the final produce to differentiate between the contribution of male and female in final production as fully separable identities (Picture 3.2).

Wright and Pollert (2005) made a survey in 50 small hotels, restaurants, bars, canteen and caterings in three English regions (London, the West Midlands and the South West) to examine the experiences of ethnic minority and migrant hotel workers in these regions. They found that about one-fourth of total female workers are cleaners or domestics, nearly a fifth are waitresses and almost one in ten is receptionists. Men are most likely to be chefs or cooks, waiters, managers or porters. Similarly in restaurants, women are much less likely to work as chefs or cooks, and are most likely to be waitresses. And in canteens and catering, half of women are kitchen and catering assistants, and are less likely to be chefs or cooks or managers than men.

Works in hotel and restaurant is characterised as low pay, low status work, exploitation of employees, low levels of unionisation and poor employment relations practices (Gabriel 1988; Price 1994; Head and Lucas 2004).

Average levels of earning in hotels and catering are low. Male full-time manual employees in hotels and restaurants earn less than the gross hourly rate for full-time manual males nationally for UK. For women the average is slightly higher, but this reflects women's lower pay generally (Smith and Carroll 2003). As more than half of employees in the sector work part-time basis and part-time hourly earnings are generally lower than full-time, these figures will underestimate the extent of low pay in the sector.

Large numbers of workers in the hotel and catering sector earn less than the lower earnings limit for paying National Insurance contributions, therefore losing out on entitlement to many state benefits such as sick pay, maternity pay, retirement pension etc. (Purcell et al. 1999).

Average weekly working hours are lower in hotel and restaurant sector than the other sectors of the UK economy, as the number of part-time workers is high in this sector. 25 % of workers in hotel and 36 % in restaurants worked less than 20 h a week. But there also exists high proportions (3.4 % in hotel and restaurant) working more than 65 h a week (Smith and Carroll 2003).

Women are more likely to work shorter hours of work than men in this sector. About 30 % of women worker in hotel, 43 % in restaurants, and 34 % in canteens and catering worked less than 20 h a week, while the corresponding figure for the men are 18 % in hotel, 26 % in restaurant and 8 % in canteens and catering. Also, the working hour of both men and women workers were lower than the national average (Wright and Pollert 2005).

Wood (1997) pointed out the reasons for the existence of small number of union in this sector as: prevalence of high levels of part-timers, seasonal and casual workers with high staff turnover; the isolation and ethos of hotel and catering work; management attitudes towards trade unions; and the role of trade unions themselves in the sector, often not seeming to make the sector a priority. Besides, Macaulay and Wood (1992) observed widespread ignorance by employees of union activity in hotels and catering, as well as employer and management hostility towards unions.

The working environment in the hotel and catering sector is often very poor. It includes many physical hazards like risk of exposure to smoke, noise and high temperature (Smith and Carroll 2003).

According to the Health and Safety Executive (HSE), many serious accidents occur in the industry. Slips, trips and falls on wet or contaminated floors are the common causes of injury. Other causes includes manual handling/musculoskeletal injuries; exposure to hot or harmful substances (e.g. hot oil, or cleaning chemicals); and being struck by something (e.g. sharp knives or falling objects). The main causes of occupational ill health continue to be: dermatitis; chronic ill health effects from manual handling; and work-related upper limb disorders. An HSE report on small firms (2002) indicated that health and safety is not viewed as a high priority by most employers in the sector. The employers think that the risks are perceived to be low because they are similar to those encountered in a domestic situation. Many small firms feel their business is too small for health and safety to be a problem (Wright and Pollert 2005).

Among the different sectors where skilled labour is engaged, health sector is a primary example. In the health sector, females are employed mostly as nursing staff in the hospitals.[4] Females are also employed as helpers and 'aayas', sometimes as washing women. They are often poorly represented in other categories, e.g. physicians, dentists, pharmatists and managers (WHO 2008). However, even in this case, the duty separability does not lend itself to labour separability. The final utility that a patient gets from a hospital is a combination of not only the

[4] Though in the present there are a number of female doctors, their percentage is still insignificant (WHO 2008).

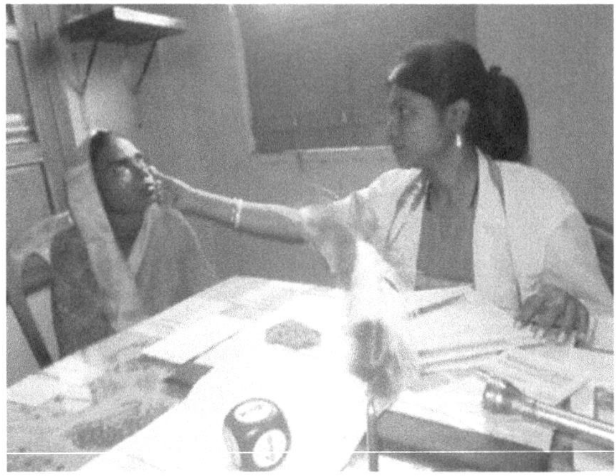

Picture 3.3 Lady doctor in a private chamber

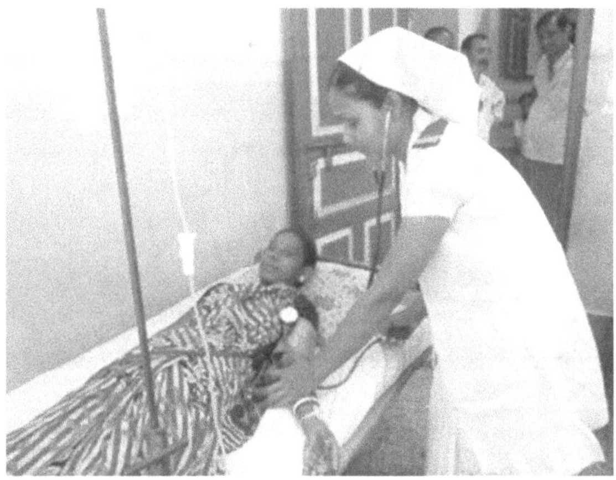

Picture 3.4 An untrained nurse in a small privately owned Nursing home

physician's service but also the behaviour of other hospital staff, mostly the nursing staff (Pictures 3.3, 3.4).

Historically the relationship between doctors (mostly male) and nurses (mostly female) followed a simple hierarchy: doctors are superior to nurses. Doctors were responsible for all the medical works for curing the patients and nurses were merely 'in charge of folding pillow cases and mopping brows' (Radcliffe 2000). Nurses' main job was nurturing patients and they had to bear in mind the professional dominance of the male doctors. But after the 1970s the role and status of nursing began to be modified through the process of professionalism and university qualifications. They offered advice, stood up to doctors and were regarded with much more respect than they previously had been (Stein et al. 1990; Williamson 2003). They also moved into administrative and supervisory positions and began to control their own licensing processes. But some argued that 'these extra responsibilities and status symbols have been delegated down by physicians to share the workload rather than to establish parity of influence (Fagin and Garelick 2004).

Picture 3.5 A lady teacher in a privately owned nursery school

Nursing still remains subordinate to medicine, but the status of the profession has changed. Nurses exercise overt autonomy (though limited) beyond their passive role. At the same time people's attitude towards doctors has also changed. 'The blurring of boundaries between 'cure' and 'care' has led to the empowerment of the nursing profession and encouraged a move to a more mutually respectful relationship between doctors and nurses' (Germov and Freij 2009).

The last example that we give is that from the education sector. In the unorganised private education sector the separability issue rarely exists even in the case of duty separability. Female teachers are employed side by side with male teachers. Even the office staff may be female. In the education institution the general societal view is that females are more suitable for teaching the kids because of their caring nature. However in higher private coaching centers, the proportion of females drastically falls. This is a sector where only partial separability may be applied because the male and females are doing almost the same duty (Picture 3.5).

Drudy et al. (2005) pointed to the common belief of men 'naturally' wanting to go into technical careers in science and technology while care giving activities are viewed as 'natural female' trait. This has led to a social construction where primary teacher becomes synonymous to 'female' and 'mother' (Smith 2004). Cortina and San Roman (2006) have given the example of Costa Rica, Spain or Mexico where wives, mothers and daughters were supplemented with male teachers with the belief that presence of a woman teacher to complement a man was needed in order to contribute maternal qualities as 'social mothers'. Based on a study of teacher training institutions in the UK, Skelton (2003) found that male student-cum-teachers largely believe that primary teaching is best suited to a women's 'nature' and this perception explain why there were smaller number of men going into the profession.

Rosemberg (2006) found that in Brazil, within the teaching profession gender disparity exists in pay with women being concentrated in low-paid pre-school and elementary sectors, while male teachers were disproportionately represented in the higher paid upper secondary and higher education. She identified this as a pattern of gender discrimination rooted within the education labour market despite the significant increase in women's education level. Feminisation of teaching profession has resulted in loss of its status within society making it largely undesirable as it also involves lower earnings and a loss of professional credibility. Mavrogeni (2005) pointed out that despite the high status of women in the teaching profession in the Cypriot economy, it shaped the women's occupational tastes and career aspirations, stagnating the prospects for women's work to evolve into other sectors.

According to UNESCO report (2011) the proportion of female teachers in India in the schools (grade 1–12) was 39.1 % in 2006–2007. While Kerala has the highest percentage (71 %) of female teachers, in Rajasthan women are poorly represented (30 %) in the teaching profession. Primary and middle schools (class 1–8) have a higher proportion of female teachers, followed by secondary schools, and slightly lower than that in senior secondary schools. Except Kerala, urban areas have a higher percentage (65 %) of female teachers than the rural Areas (37 %). Again the proportion of female teachers in Government schools is substantially lower than in aided and unaided schools. The most striking feature is that, the proportion of female teachers in higher education is significantly low. It was only 18 % in 1993–1994.

Women's choice between school and higher education teacher is not always career-oriented. This may be due to their socialisation or constraint in choice open to them. General education has always been preferred to professional education as the latter required additional investment in coaching for entrance tests. Though recently more women are entering into the professional education, they continue to be employed in short-term, contractual low-paid jobs. Besides the recruitment policy of different states has also determined the extent to which women were able to access the teaching profession. For example, Bihar Govt. decided that no teacher should be employed within the 15 km of their residence. This is particularly difficult for a female teacher, since in a patriarchal society it is female teacher's husband's location that determines the location of the family.

Educational policy in post-independence India has given much stress on the recruitment of female teachers to draw girls into school. In gender segregated societies, the presence of female teachers gives the required assurance to the parents of the well-being and safety of their daughters.

References

Barnabas AJ, Arnabasu DC, Paul S (2009) A Study on the empowerment of women construction workers as masons in Tamil Nadu, India, J Int Women's Stud 11(2):121–141

Baruah B (2010) Women and globalisation: challenges and opportunities facing construction workers in contemporary India. Dev Pract 20(1):31–44

Becker GS (1975) Human capital, 2nd edn. Columbia University Press, New York

Becker G (1985) Human capital, effort and sexual division of labor. J Labor Econ 3(1):33–58

Bergman BR (1974) Occupational segregation, wages and profits when employers discriminate by race and sex. Eastern Econ J 1:103–110 April–July

Blau F, Ferber M, Winkler A (1998) The economics of women, men and work, 3rd edn. Prentice Hall, Upper Saddle River
Boserup E (1970) Woman's role in economic development. St. Martin's Press, New York
Cairnes JE (1874) Some leading principles of political economy—newly expounded. Harpar and Brothers, New York
Chodorow N (1974) Family structure and feminine personality. In: Rosaldo M, Lamphere L (eds) Woman culture and society. Stanford, California
Coontz S, Henderson P (1986) Women's work, men's property: the origins of gender and class. Verso, London
Cortina R, San Roman S (2006) Women and teaching: global perspectives on the feminisation of a profession. Palgrave and Macmillan, New York
Deolalikar AB, Vijverberg WPM (1987) A Test of heterogeneity of family and hired labor in Asian agriculture. Oxford Bull Econ Stat 49(3):291–305
DN and GK (1989) Sexual division of labour. Econ Polit Wkly 24(34):1949–1950
Drudy S, Martin M, Woods M, O'Flynn J (2005) Men and the classroom: gender imbalances in teaching. Routledge, New York
Duncan G (1976) Earnings functions and nonpecuniary benefits. J Human Resour 11(4):462–483
Fagin L, Garelick A (2004) The doctor–nurse relationship. Adv Psychiatr Treat 10:277–286
Gabriel Y (1988) Working lives in catering. Routledge, London
Germov J, Freij M (2009) Second opinion 4th (edn). Online Case Studies
Gunderson M (1975) Male-female wage differentials and the impact of equal pay legislation. Rev Econ Stat 57(1):462–469
Gunderson M (1989) Male-female wage differentials and policy responses. J Econ Lit 27(1):46–72
Habib I (2008) Medieval India: the study of a civilization. National Book Trust, New Delhi
Hakim C (2000) Preference theory: work lifestyle choices in the 21st century. Oxford University press, Oxford
Head J, Lucas R (2004) Employee relations in the non-union hotel industry: a case of "determined opportunism"? Pers Rev 33(6):693–710
Long J (1995) The effects of taste and motivation on individual income. Ind Labor Relat Rev 48(2):338–351
Mavrogeni LE (2005) The feminisation of the teaching profession in Cyprus M.A. Dissertation, Institute of Education, University of London
Macaulay IR, Wood CR (1992) Hotel and Catering Industry Employees' Attitudes towards Trade Unions. Empl Relat 14(3):20–28
Mukhopadhyay CC, Higgins PJ (1988) Anthropological studies of women's status revisited: 1977–1987. Annu Rev Anthropol 17:461–495
Muredock GP (1968) Discussion. In: Lee RB, Devor I (ed) Man the Hunter, Chicago
Oaxaca R (1973) Male-female wage differentials in urban labor markets. Int Econ Rev 14(3):693–709
Paarsch HJ, Shearer BS (2004) Male Female productivity differentials: the role of ability and incentives, (mimeo). Department of Economics, University of Iowa, Iowa
Parr J (1988) Disaggregating the sexual division of labour: a transatlantic case study. Comp Stud Soc Hist 30(3):511–533
Price L (1994) Poor personnel practice in the hotel and catering industry: does it matter? Human Resour Manag J 4(4):44–62
Purcell K, McKnight A, Simm C (1999) The lower earnings limit in practice: part-time employment in hotels and catering. Equal Opportunities Commission, Manchester
Radcliffe M (2000) Doctors and nurses: new game, same result. Br Med J 320(7241):1085
Rani U, Unni J (1999) Urban informal sector: size and income generation processes in gujarat. SEWA, Ahmedabad
Rosaldo M (1974) Woman, culture and society: a theoretical overview. In: Rosaldo M, Lamphere L (eds) Woman, culture and society. Stanford University Press, Stanford
Rosemburg F (2006) Educational policies and gender: an assessment of the 1990s in Brazil. In: Cortina and San Roman (eds) Women and teaching: global perspectives on the feminisation of a profession, Palgrave MacMillan, New York

Sen J (1966) Ethnographic notes on the Birhor. Bull Anthropol Survey India 14(1/2):45–58
Skelton C (2003) Male primary teachers and perceptions of masculinity. Educ Rev 55(2):195–209
Smith J (2004) Male primary teachers: Disadvantaged or advantaged? Paper presented to the Australian association for research in education conference, Melbourne (Dec)
Smith M, Carroll M (2003) Branch report for hotel and restaurants in the UK, in Klein Hesselink J (2004) EU hotel and restaurant sector: work and employment conditions, Unpublished, European Foundation for the improvement of living and working conditions: Dublin.
Stein LI, Watts DT, Howell T (1990) The doctor-nurse game revisited. N Engl J Med 322:546–549
Thurrow LC (1969) Poverty and discrimination. Brooking Institution, Washington DC
UNESCO (2011) Women and the teaching profession: exploring the feminisation debate. London, UK and Paris, France
Vaid KN (1999) (ed) Women in Construction. NICMAR Publication Bureau, Mumbai
Webb S, Webb B (1897) Industrial democracy. Longmans and Green, London
Williamson M (2003) Challenging doctors' orders: in order to provide good care to children and their families, nurses sometimes need to challenge doctors' decisions. The Free Library (1 Oct) http://www.thefreelibrary.com/Challenging.doctors'.orders:in.order.to.provide.good.careto-a0114702096
Wise D (1975) Academic achievement and job performance. Am Econ Rev 65(3):350–366
Wood RC (1997) Working in hotels and catering, 2nd edn. International Thomson Business Press, London
WHO (2008) Spotlight on statistics—a fact file on health workforce statistics Issue No.2. Gender and Health Workforce Statistics
Wright T, Pollert A (2005) The experience of ethnic minority workers in the hotel and catering industry: routes to support and advice on workplace problems. Working paper 1, Working Lives Research Institute, London Metropolitan University

Chapter 4
Framework of Study

4.1 General Model

In order to assess male female differential across different types of enterprises, we consider a simple production function of the type:

$$y = g(K, L(L_f, L_m)) \tag{4.1}$$

where K is the capital stock and L the labour input that is a function of female labour input (L_f) and male labour input (L_m). The exact form of the labour input function will depend on the assumption of separability.

Under perfect separability (JS model),[1] it is possible to write down:

$$L(L_f, L_m) = \varphi(L_f)\delta(L_m) \tag{4.2}$$

The production function can be written simply as:

$$y = f(K, L_f, L_m) \tag{4.3}$$

In this case, the shadow wages (or marginal products) are (Jacoby 1992, 1993; Skoufias 1994; Abdulai and Regmi 2000):

$$w_f^* = \frac{\partial y}{\partial L_f} \tag{4.4a}$$

and

$$w_m^* = \frac{\partial y}{\partial L_m} \tag{4.4b}$$

these shadow wages reflect male-female productivity differential in the perfect separability case.

[1] This is the model that is studied by Jacoby (1992, 1993), Skoufias (1994), Abdulai and Regmi (2000). Henceforth we will term it as the Jacoby-Skoufias (JS) model.

A. Sengupta et al., *Productivity, Separability and Deprivation*,
SpringerBriefs in Economics, DOI: 10.1007/978-81-322-1056-6_4,

Under partial separability (DV model)[2] functional form such as (4.2) is non-existent. Assuming that the labour input function is linear homogeneous, it is possible to derive:

$$L(L_f, L_m) = L(L_f, L - L_f) = L_1(L, L_f) = LL_1(1, L_f/L) = LL_2(L_f/L) = LL_2(\lambda) \tag{4.5}$$

The production function may be rewritten as:

$$y = g(K, LL_2(\lambda))$$

Assuming the function to be linear homogeneous

$$y/L = g(K/L, L_2(\lambda)) = h(K/L, \lambda) \tag{4.6}$$

where λ is the proportion of female labour to total labour. In order to estimate labour productivity it is necessary to specify the relevant functional forms. We take this exercise in the following subsections.

4.2 Partial Separability

Numerous forms have been assumed for the labour function. These various forms are basically assumed to be linear homogeneous type.[3] On this basis it is possible to write the function in the form:

$$L(L_f, L_m) = LL_2(\lambda) \tag{4.7}$$

Following Ghosh and Neogi (1996) we assume (4.5) to be of a linear additive type:

$$L = \theta L_m + (1 - \theta)L_f. \tag{4.8}$$

where L_f and L_m represent the number of female and male labourers respectively employed in OAE and Establishments and θ represents the quality parameter so that $0 < \theta < 1$. The weighted average (linear combination) of the female and male labourers employed in the two sectors allows only a quality differential.

---

[2] This model is studied by Deolalikar and Vijverberg (1987), Ghosh and Neogi (1996), Chattapadhyay and Sharma (2001). We can term it as Deolalikar-Vijverberg (DV) model.

[3] Deolalikar and Vijverberg (1987) assumed the function to be of additive type. The model was also used by Ghosh and Neogi (1996). This specification allows direct estimation of the labour productivity in the partial separability case. Chattopadhyay and Sharma (2001) however assume the function to be a CES type. Such a functional form allows us to measure the degree of substitutability between male and female labour. However since the function is non-linear, the estimates become unreliable without proper identification restrictions. This prompted us to use the additive form.

We also considered a production function of standard *C-D* type[4] where only two inputs, labor (*L*) and capital (*K*) produce a single output (*y*) so that

$$y = AK^{\alpha}L^{\beta} \tag{4.9}$$

Assuming that there is no quality differential between capitals in the two sectors Eq. (4.9) can be written as:

$$\begin{aligned} y &= AK^{\alpha}[\theta L_m + (1-\theta)L_f]^{\beta} \\ &= AK^{\alpha}[\theta(L - L_f) + (1-\theta)L_f]^{\beta} \text{ since } L = L_f + L_m \\ &= AK^{\alpha}[\theta L - \theta L_f + (1-\theta)L_f]^{\beta} \\ &= AK^{\alpha}(\theta L)^{\beta}[1 + \{(1-\theta)/\theta\}L_f/L - L_f/L]^{\beta} \\ &= AK^{\alpha}\theta^{\beta}L^{\beta}[1 + \{(1-\theta)/\theta - 1\}L_f/L]^{\beta} \\ &= AK^{\alpha}\theta^{\beta}L^{\beta}[1 + (\gamma - 1)L_f/L]^{\beta} \end{aligned} \tag{4.10}$$

where $\gamma = (1-\theta)/\theta$

Taking log on both sides we obtain:

$$\log y = A_0 + \alpha \log K + \beta \log L + \beta \log[1 + (\gamma - 1)L_f/L] \tag{4.11}$$

with $A_0 = \log A + \beta \log \theta$

Now if male and female labour in the informal service sector are equally productive then the value of the parameter θ would be 0.5 which implies that $\gamma = 1$. On the other hand if the male workers in OAE and Establishments are more productive than those of female workers then the value of $\theta > 0.5$ which implies that $\gamma < 1$ and the reverse is true when $\gamma > 1$. In our exercise, we have estimated the coefficients of Eq. (4.11) directly by the nonlinear Maximum likelihood method and test for the value of γ, where the null hypothesis is H_0: $\gamma = 1$ and the alternative hypothesis is H_1: $\gamma < 1$.

4.3 Perfect Separability

The basic assumption in this model is a utility maximizing productive unit[5] that consumes leisure, home goods and market produced goods (Jacoby 1992, 1993; Skoufias 1994; Abdulai and Regmi 2000).

$$U = U(C, T_f^e, T_m^e, Z) \tag{4.12}$$

[4] The Cobb-Douglas form has a number of limitations. However use of more flexible functional forms (such as translog) yielded results that were inconclusive. Moreover Jacoby's (1993) study show that though the quantitative results become sensitive to functional specifications, qualitative results are, more or less, unaffected.

[5] The model is useful in comparing the OAE and Establishment units under informal service sector. OAEs are mostly family enterprises making the analysis appropriate. Arguing that family labour is used even in the Establishment units, the model can capture sufficient amount of reality.

where T_f^e and T_m^e are the leisure enjoyed by female and male members, C is the total consumption that is the sum of home produced goods (Q) and market purchased goods (G) while Z captures certain family characteristics. The budget constraint is given by the amount of market good that is purchased from the market. This in turn depends on family's income. Jacoby (1993) assumes that the income has three components: (1) net profit from family business (Π) (2) labour income from hiring out family member (*FML*) and (3) household's non-farm non-labour income net of fixed costs (V). Symbolically the budget constraint is:

$$G = \Pi + FML + V \tag{4.13}$$

Now it is clear that these components of (4.13) depend on a set of parameters. Net profit from family business (Π) is determined among other things by the volume of marketed goods (y). Similarly, labour income (*FML*) depends on the running market wage (w). Lastly, household's net non-labour income (V) can be assessed from the volume of home goods (Q). In effect thus, the productive unit faces two types of production functions. The production function for the good that the unit sells in the market is given as:

$$y = f(K, L_f, L_m, E) \tag{4.14}$$

The equation is basically the same as (4.3) with E representing some fixed inputs that are relevant for producing y. Similarly one can describe home goods' production function as:

$$Q = Q(S_m, S_f, A) \tag{4.15}$$

where S_i is the amount of labour of the type i $(i = f, m)$ which is used in home production and A is vector of fixed inputs necessary for home production.

A productive unit is assumed to maximize the utility function (4.12) given the budget constraint (4.13) that incorporates both the production functions (Eqs. 4.14 and 4.15). It is assumed that the commodity y (that is either produced by the firm or purchased from the market) is perfectly substitutable with home produced goods Q.[6] The first order conditions for this problem state that labourers equate their marginal rate of substitution between consumption and leisure or shadow wage either to their market wage or to their marginal product in either farm work or housework. The decision of a labourer to participate in the labour market depends on the shadow wage[7] and the income net of such shadow costs. In the home production literature this is defined as full income.

---

[6] This is the standard assumption made by all the authors (Jacoby 1992, 1993; Skoufias 1994; Abdulai and Regmi 2000). The unit is assumed to have no preference for home produced goods.

[7] They are already defined in Eqs. (4.4a) and (4.4b).

By envelope theorem, the maximum profits are functions of input prices. For family labour, these input prices are indexed by shadow wages. This then generates the labour supply functions:

$$L_i^* = L_i^* \left(w_f^*, w_m^*, \hat{V}; Z \right) \tag{4.16}$$

where $\hat{V}$ is the optimum amount of V and the vector Z is the set of exogenous factors (such as social norms) that affects labour supply decisions.

For empirical estimation of the model there had hardly been any data regarding home production. Hence we concentrated only on the firm production side of these sectors. In this case the production function will be:

$$y = AK^{\alpha} L_f^{\beta_1} L_m^{\beta_2} \tag{4.17}$$

Following Jacoby (1993), the shadow wage rates (or marginal products) of male and female labourers are calculated from the estimates of Cobb-Douglas production function[8] using the formula:

$$\hat{w}_i = \frac{\hat{\beta}_i \hat{y}_i}{L_i} \quad i = M, F \tag{4.18}$$

However even then there exists considerable difference between actual income and full income.[9] It is interesting to see how woman participation rate (ratio of female labour to total labour) is influenced by the above factors.[10]

4.4 Justification for Using Cobb-Douglas Function

An important problem of econometric analysis of the production process is the choice of appropriate production function. Lots of debates have been raised, arguments provided and justification emerged for and against the choice of a particular production function. In fact this is a veritable battle ground for competitive ideas and viewpoints. However it is never possible to find a functional form that would

[8] Since the inputs themselves are likely to be endogenously determined (Abdulai and Regmi 2000), we have used instrumental variable method rather than simple OLS to estimate the production function. OLS method may give biased estimates.

[9] For example Sen (1964) argued that if we value the family labour according to their market wage, most of the firms would become unremunerative. He suggested the use of shadow price that could appropriately capture such situation.

[10] There has been a considerable debate in this regard. Skoufias (1994) has found a backward bending labour supply curve for Indian females while Rosenweig (1980) found such a relationship for Indian males. In contrast, Jacoby (1993) found a positive labour supply curve for Peru. Abdulai and Regmi (2000) found a similar relationship in rural Nepal.

be free from all the deficiencies that the theorists wish it to be. Hence the choice of functional form is always pragmatic depending on the problem to be studied, data availability and the background realities.

Among the functional forms that are generally used for empirical studies concerning industry, the Cobb-Douglas form is the most popular one (Goldar 1997). The Cobb-Douglas function has various desirable properties, such as homogeneity, convexity and diminishing returns to factors. The form is also very suitable for measuring various types of output elasticities directly from the data. The function is popular in cross-sectional, time series and panel data study. It has a long history of empirical application ever since its inception by Cobb and Douglas (1928).

Solow (1957), Denison (1962) and Jorgenson (1963) popularized the use of the Cobb-Douglas function in estimating the aggregate production function of the economy and its various dynamics. They have shown that the Cobb-Douglas function may be suitably used in understanding the changes in technical progress and its origin empirically. However it would be a long history to state the entire development. Further it may not be appropriate for the problem at our hand. It would be better to concentrate on a few recent studies particularly those dealing with the Indian experience and/or the analysis of the service sector.

The analyses by Ahluwalia (1991) and Goldar (1997) were the two important studies on Indian industry that used the Cobb-Douglas function. In both the studies it has been found that the estimates of the return to scale parameter are not significantly different from one so that the CRS hypothesis cannot be rejected. The estimates of these studies reveal that the overall explanatory power of the Cobb-Douglas function is high.

However Goldar (1997) argued that there might be some problem of multicollinearity and serial correlation of the disturbance term affecting the reliability of the estimates of the Cobb-Douglas function. Some of the latter techniques have been proposed by Barua and Leech (1987).

A standard argument against the Cobb-Douglas function is that the estimation of the function by OLS may yield biased and inconsistent estimates because the disturbance term of the production function is dependent on the choice of input (Goldar 1997). One way to solve this problem may be the use of joint estimation of the production function along with the input demand function. Even this procedure has a number of limitations. However the derivation of the income share equation involves the assumption that the factors are paid according to their marginal product (Goldar 1997). The violation of this assumption may lead to serious discrepancies yielding biased result. Further Zellner (1962) established that under reasonable assumptions (both about the error term and the behavioural attitude) the inputs can be shown to be independent of the errors of the production function. In such cases the ordinary least square regression would yield consistent and unbiased estimates of the parameters of the Cobb-Douglas function.

A further argument against the Cobb-Douglas function is the essentiality of each inputs and constraining the elasticity of substitution to unity. The first argument was raised by Rudra (1982) in his study on Indian agriculture. He provided a solution to this problem. However it may be noted that this essentiality problem is not typical to Cobb-Douglas only but of any functional form that uses logarithmic transformation of the input and output variables. The second issue rules out the possibility of complementarity between inputs. However as shown by Hicks (1956) in the two input one output case as used by most econometrician, the inputs are necessarily substitutes, since they compete on the available fund of the firms. Generalising the elasticity of substitution and even making it variable is a possibility. However the complex functions that are generated often fail to give better fit than the Cobb-Douglas function, particularly if the homogeneity restrictions are imposed. In fact the Cobb-Douglas function is nested in the generalized translog form itself (Dimitriu and Savu 2010).

An interesting application of the Cobb-Douglas function to the unorganised manufacturing sector in India has been made by Dimitriu and Savu (2010), Kathuria et al (2010). Both these approaches utilised the NSS data on the unorganised manufacturing sector in India. The first study used the NSS data from 1994–1995 to 2000–2001. The study estimated technical efficiency across the sub-sector of industries as provided by the NSS two digit NIC code that the NSSO utilises. The study compares the efficiency across two time points 1994–1995 and 2000–2001 detailing both rural and urban origin. A significant finding of the study is that the industries that have not been detailed (‘other manufacturing industries’ and ‘not recorded cases’) show a higher level of efficiency than the other sub-sectors. Comparison across the two time points revealed that for a couple of industries efficiency has declined. Further efficiency is higher in urban areas irrespective of the ownership pattern. Credit is an important constraint for achieving efficiency. Among the types DME’s are most efficient followed by NDME and OAME’s.

Kathuria et al. (2010) studied the efficiency dynamics in a different dimension. They considered inter-state performance rather than inter-sectoral differences. Also total factor productivity growth has been measured across three time points (1994–1995, 2000–2001, 2005–2006). Using a Cobb-Douglas structure they calculated the total factor productivity (TFP) across the time points. Interestingly the study finds that considering the overall period (1994–2006) almost all the states have both negative GVA growth and TFPG. For GVA growth the exceptional states are Haryana, Rajasthan, West Bengal and Madhya Pradesh. For TFPG the exceptional states are UP and Madhya Pradesh. Thus Madhya Pradesh is the only state that has both positive GVA growth and TFP growth. This may be easily explained by the low initial level of achievement of Madhya Pradesh and its current revival from such an abysmal condition.

Now we consider some studies that deal with the application of Cobb-Douglas function in the service sector. An important work on the condition of service sector in South Korea is done by Park and Sanidas (2011). The study estimates the TFP growth that is generated in the Korean service sector. For empirical estimates KLEMS (Capital, Labour, Energy, Materials and Services) production function framework is used that includes capital, labour intermediate inputs and other control variables. Thus they used the augmented Cobb-Douglas function popularised by Cainelli (2008). Here besides the traditional inputs the authors utilised some controlled variables in the production function structure. The use of the function was necessary, because they utilized the industry level data in their empirical analysis. Empirical analysis show that the service sector has been more affected by a services input than manufacturing sector has. The controlled variables also influence the output. The study analyses the impact of the financial crises and finds substantial effect on the performance of this sector.

There are also some studies that analyses the tourism sector using the Cobb-Douglas specification. We briefly mention only two studies. El-Mooty and El-Shawadfy (2007) have used a physical and a monetary Cobb-Douglas function for the Egyptian tourism sector. For the physical model they used variables measured in physical units (such as output in no. of tourist nights, capital in no. of tourist rooms etc.). The data was available for 19 years (1982–2000). The monetary model used the value of the variables instead of their physical units (such as GDP in tourism sector per year, wages of workers etc.). The data was available for 40 years (1960–2000). The analysis clearly reveals that the monetary data is a better fit than the physical model. The authors argued that "C-D production function in monetary model may be good formula in service sectors" (El-Mooty and El-Shawadfy 2007).

Another study on services is an analysis of South African tourism. The report utilized C-D specification for a period of 8 years (2001–2007). The study considers both domestic and foreign tourist expenditure. It argues that the C-D production function has been the standard workhorse in empirical studies in South Africa (and many other countries). Two inputs capital and labour are used with technology as the residual. The analysis reveals certain differences between domestic and foreign tourist expenditure on both fixed capital formation and employment. Domestic tourism expenditure has a significantly higher impact than the foreign expenditure. Also the elasticities confirm the operation of constant return to scale (CRS).

Reviewing the above literature briefly clearly indicates that the C-D form is widely used in analysing both agricultural and unorganised industrial sector and also the service sector. The advantage of using this function is its tractability and interpretational simplicity. Our study deals with the study of the unorganised service sector in India. This sector has a high level of technological flexibility and substitutability unlike the large organized units. Further it generally depicts a picture of low profitability and little scope for expanding the units (Banerjee and Dufflo 2011). As Banerjee and Dufflo (2011) argue, these people suffer from serious asset constraints and lack of accessibility to formal market credit (Chap. 6, pp. 133–155). There are only a few cases where a profitable expansion of the sector has been possible. It is in this context that the C-D function may be more appropriate for analysing the small unprofitable units, facing serious credit constraints and very little prospect of flowering to a full phased profitable enterprise.

References

Abdulai A, Regmi PP (2000) Estimating labor supply of farm households under non-separability: empirical evidence from Nepal. Agr Econ 22(3):309–320

Ahluwalia IJ (1991) Productivity and growth in Indian manufacturing. Oxford University Press, New Delhi

Banerjee AV, Duflo E (2011) Poor economics: a radical rethinking of the way to fight global poverty. Random House, India

Barua A, Leech D (1987) Factor substitution and returns to scale in Indian manufacturing: a cross-section analysis. Discussion paper, international trade and development division, school of international studies, Jawaharlal Nehru University, New Delhi

Cainelli G (2008) Spatial agglomeration, technological innovations, and firm productivity: evidence from Italian industrial districts. Growth Change 39(3):414–435

Chattapadhyay M, Sharma CS (2001) Is labor homogeneous quantity in Indian agriculture. Mimeo, Indian Statistical Institute, Kolkata

Cobb CW, Douglas PH (1928) A theory of production. Am Econ Rev 18(1):139–165 March

Denison EF (1962) The sources of economic growth in the United States and the alternatives before Us. Committee Econ Dev, New York

Deolalikar AB, Vijverberg WPM (1987) A Test of heterogeneity of family and hired labor in Asian agriculture. Oxford Bull Econ Stat 49(3):291–305

Dimitriu MC, Savu BM (2010) Econometric analysis of efficiency in the Indian manufacturing sector. Rom J Econ Forecast 1:182–197

El-Moaty KA, El-Shawadfy M (2007) An Estimation of Cobb-Douglas production function in Egyptian Tourism Sector, Zagazig University. Source: interstat.statjournals.net/Year/2007/articles/0705003.pdf

Ghosh B, Neogi C (1996) Liberalisation in India: quality differentials between public and private employees. Dev Econ 34(1):61–79

Goldar BN (1997) Econometrics of Indian industry. In: Krishna KL (ed) Econometric applications in India. Oxford University Press, New Delhi

Hicks JR (1956) A revision of demand theory. Clarendon, Oxford

Jacoby HG (1992) Productivity of men and women and the sexual division of labor in peasant agriculture of the Peruvian Sierra. J Dev Econ 37:265–287

Jacoby HG (1993) Shadow wages and peasant family labor supply; an econometric application to the Peruvian Sierra. Rev Econ Stud 60:903–921

Jorgenson DW (1963) Capital theory and investment behavior. Am Econ Rev 53(2):247–259

Kathuria V, Natarajan RRS, Sen K (2010) Fluctuating productivity performance of unorganised manufacturing in the post 1990s. Indian J Labour Econ 53(2):285–303

Park H, Sanidas E (2011) Korean augmented production function: the role of services and other factors in Korea's economic growth of industries. J Econ Dev 36(1):59–85

Rosenweig MR (1980) Neoclassical theory and the optimizing peasant: an econometric analysis of market family labour supply in a developing country. Q J Econ 94(1):31–55

Rudra A (1982) Indian agricultural economics: myths and realities. Allied, New Delhi

Sen AK (1964) Size of holdings and productivity. The Economic Weekly 16 (5-7) Annual number, February: 323–326

Skoufias E (1994) Using shadow wages to estimate labor supply of agricultural households. Am J Agric Econ 76(2):215–227

Solow RM (1957) Technical change and the aggregate production function. Rev Econ Stat 39(3):312–320 August

Zellner A (1962) An efficient method of estimating seemingly unrelated regressions and tests for aggregate bias. J Am Stat Assoc 57(298):348–368

Chapter 5
Data Used

5.1 Preliminary Ideas

For our study we have used the 57th round data of National Sample Survey Organisation (NSSO) pertaining to the period 2001–2002. This round collected detailed information on economic and operational characteristics of unorganized service sector enterprises (excluding trade and finance) in addition to data on household consumer expenditure and employment-unemployment in India.

Geographical Coverage: The survey covered all the thirty-five states and union territories of India in both rural and urban areas. It did not include (1) Leh and Kargil districts of Jammu and Kashmir, (2) Villages situated beyond 5 kms. of bus route in the state of Nagaland, (3) Villages of Andaman and Nicobar Islands that remain inaccessible throughout the year and (4) 202 villages and 11 UFS (Urban Frame Survey) blocks where economic census of 1998 could not be conducted.

Sampling Design: A stratified multi-stage design was followed for the survey. The first stage units (FSUs) were villages (Panchayat wards for Kerala) in rural areas and urban frame survey (UFS) blocks (wards of 61 towns of Karnataka) in urban areas. The ultimate stage units (USUs) were enterprises and households. Larger FSUs were divided into hamlet groups (hg) and sub-blocks (sb).

Total number of sample FSUs selected in each state and UTs was in proportion to the number of workers in unorganised sector enterprises engaged in the activities listed under the economic census 1998. Then samples were allocated to rural and urban sectors in proportion to the total number of workers in each sector. The rural/urban sample was further allocated to the various strata in proportion to the total numbers of workers. FSUs were selected from the sub-strata by circular systematic sampling (CSS) with probability, proportional to size (PPS) where the size of an FSU is determined by the number of workers in the FSU. At last enterprises were selected from FSUs by applying SRSWOR, for detailed enquiry.

A. Sengupta et al., *Productivity, Separability and Deprivation*,
SpringerBriefs in Economics, DOI: 10.1007/978-81-322-1056-6_5,

This round of NSSO included the following types of enterprises:

1. All the enterprises except units registered under section 2m (i) and 2m (ii) of Factories act, 1948 and Bidi and Cigar Workers (condition of employment) Act 1966.
2. All enterprises except those run by Government (Central Government, State Government, Local bodies)/Public Sector Enterprises.

The different activities of unorganized service sector covered in this survey along with the corresponding NIC group/class/sub-class are given in the Table 5.1. A group has been mentioned if all the activities within that group were covered. If all activities under a group were not covered, the particular sub-classes under survey are mentioned.

Let us consider a brief description of the activities covered in the survey.

Hotels: A 'hotel' is an enterprise that provides lodging services with and without meal arrangement and refreshments. Dharmasala, private guest house, hostels, messes, tourist lodges, hostels for students and working girls etc. were also included in this category. Similar facilities provided by YMCA (Young Men's Christian Association), R. K. Mission, Lions club, Rotary club etc. to its workers were also considered. But facilities provided by Govt., PSU and statutory bodies (ISI, IIT, Universities etc.) were not considered.

Restaurants: A 'restaurant' is one which provides eating and drinking services for immediate consumption without lodging provision. Bars and other drinking places were also considered as restaurants. Canteens located in factories, offices were also included in this category, if they were run by private contractors.

Table 5.1 Activities covered in the survey and their NIC group/class/sub-class

Sl. No.	Activity/group	Sub-class	NIC 1998 codes
1.	Hotel and restaurant (H)	Hotel (H1)	551
		Restaurant (H2)	552
2.	Transport, storage and communication (I)	Storage and warehousing (I1)	6302
		Mechanised road transport (I2)	6021, 60221, 60231
		Other transport and related activities (I3)	601, 60222, 60232, 61, 6301, 6303, 6304, 6309
		Communication (I4)	64
3.	Real estate, renting and business activities (K)		70, 71, 72, 73, 74
4.	Education (M)		80
5.	Health and social work (N)		85
6.	Other community, social and personal services (O)		90, 911, 9191, 92, 93

Source NSSO

Storage and Warehousing: Such services which are used on hire by farm producer, traders, processor and manufacturing enterprises are termed as 'storage and warehousing'. Farm products included potato, fruits, dairy products, fish, oilseeds, jute, tobacco etc. whereas manufactured products included textiles, machine tools apparatus and equipment. But products stored by the owner of a firm or dealer or a manufacturer in his own godown or warehouse are excluded.

Transport: 'Transport' is defined as an activity that carries passengers and goods with a business motive. Supporting services such as packing, freighting travel agency etc. are included under transport. Transport services include transport by bus, tramways, other motor vehicles, freight transport by motor vehicles or any other road transport by mechanised vehicles. Within the 'other transport and related activities' the following activities were covered: (1) Carriage by bullock-cart/ekka/tonga etc. (2) transport by animals like horses, elephants, mules, camels, etc. (3) transport by rickshaw-pullers, cart operators, etc. (4) all kinds of water transport, (5) supporting transport services such as toll booths, parking lots, traffic on highway bridges, etc. (6) supporting services to water transport like operation and maintenance of piers, docks, light houses, loading and discharging vessels, etc.

Communication: Communication services includes courier services, ISD/STD/PCO booths, voice mail services through computer networking, Video/fax services, voiced and non voiced leased circuits, telex/FAX/data services through computer network, radio paging, audio services and services of cable operators, cellular agencies etc.

Real estate, Renting and Business Activities: Within this category following services were included: (1) purchase, sale, letting and operating of real estate (both residential and non-residential buildings, (2) developing and sub-dividing real estate into lots, (3) lessors of real property, (4) real estate agents, brokers and managers engaged in renting, buying and selling, managing real estate on a contact basis, (5) renting of machinery and equipment.

Education: Educational institutions are covered under this category. Research and scientific services on biological, physical and social sciences, meterological institutes, computer training centres, nursing schools, schools of music, drama, dance, fine arts, modeling, fashion designing, yoga, physical education and general coaching centres for various competitive examinations were also covered. All educational institutions not recognised by central/state/local Govts./autonomous bodies like AICTE, IIT, University etc. were covered. Similar services provided by YMCA, R.K. Mission, Lions club, Rotary club etc. were also covered.

Health and Social work: Enterprises providing health and medical services came under this category. All dispensaries, clinics, consultation chambers run by doctor, veterinary hospitals, private practice by doctors and paramedical persons (midwife, dhai etc.) were included. Similar services provided by YMCA, R. K. Mission, Lions club, Rotary club etc. were also included under health and social work.

Other Community, Social and Personal Services: Activities like sewage and refuse disposal, washing and cleaning of textile products, hair dressing, beauty parlours, funeral and related services, massage saloons, sauna baths, activities of shoe shiners, porters, car parkers, activities of portrait and photographic studios, work of palmists and astrologers were included in this category. Some services, such as housemaids, cooks, gardeners, baby sitters, *chowkidars*, night watchmen etc. provided by some agencies against prescribed fees were considered as enterprises and covered under this category.

5.2 Concepts and Definitions

In this section we discuss some concepts and definitions used by the NSSO for covering the informal service sector in India.

Own Account Enterprise (OAE): An OAE is an enterprise which is run by household labour, usually without any hired worker employed on a 'fairly regular basis'. By 'fairly regular basis' it is meant that the employment was provided for a major part of the period of operation of the enterprise during the last one year.

Establishment: An enterprise that employed at least one hired worker for a major part of the year for its operation is called establishment. Hired worker included paid or unpaid apprentices, paid household member/servant/resident worker in an enterprise.

For our analysis we have considered OAE as family enterprise or traditional enterprise as it was run by purely family members without employing any hired worker and establishment as commercial enterprise as it employed hired worker for a considerable period of operation during the reference period.

Gross Value Added: It represents the actual contribution of the enterprise to the economy. It has been calculated by subtracting the total operating expenses from total receipts during the period under consideration. Total receipt is measured by the value of services provided to other concerns and the sale value of manufactured items traded with other enterprises. Operating expenses is measured by total values of raw materials, electricity, fuel, lubricants and other auxiliary materials consumed, cost of maintenance, services purchased and other expenses incurred by the enterprise.

Worker: A person who was engaged in the production activity of the enterprise, either full time or part time basis was called a worker. His contribution towards the entrepreneurial activity may be either primary or supervisory. He/she might or might not have received wages/salaries for his work. The term 'worker' might not mean that the same person was working continuously; it only referred to a position. Persons working for not more than half of the normal working hours of the enterprise on a fairly regular basis were considered to be a part-time worker. On the other hand those who were employed for more than half of the normal time were called full-time workers. Every part-time worker has been considered as a worker.

Capital: Capital was measured by fixed assets, either owned or hired. Fixed assets are those which were held either for producing goods or for providing services but were not held for resale in the normal course of entrepreneurial activity. These included all goods-old or new that had normal economic life of more than one year.

5.3 Different Features of the Data

The NSSO data gives detailed information on various characteristics like value added, types of workers, assets, loan etc. of the unorganised service sector enterprises. It also collected information on other characteristics like type of ownership, type of operation, number of months of operation, whether accounts maintained or not, whether registered, nature of problem faced, social group of owner and so on, covering all the states and union territories of India. Let us now consider some of the features of the data.

5.3.1 Total Number of Enterprises

The NSSO data covered 3.61 lakh enterprises that were operative in the unorganised service sector in India during the period 2001–2002. Of these 38 % were located in rural areas and 62 % in urban areas. It can further be seen from Table 5.2 that above 69 % of enterprises were OAE's which were operative without engaging any hired worker on a regular basis and nearly 31 % were establishment with at least one hired worker on a regular basis.

5.3.2 Region-Wise Division of States and UTs

For our analysis we have divided all the states and UTs into four regions. Region-wise division of states and UTs are presented in Fig. 5.1 as well as in Table 5.3.

5.3.3 Percentage of Enterprises in the Different Regions

The distribution of the enterprises over OAE and Establishment among the different regions of the country is shown in Fig. 5.2a, b, as our primary interest

Table 5.2 Total number of enterprises

	OAE	Establishment	All
Rural	106,200	31,914	138,114 (38.2)
Urban	145,288	78,374	223,662 (61.8)
Combined	251,488 (69.5)	110,288 (30.5)	361,776

Figures in the bracket represent percentage of total enterprises. *Source* Author's own calculations from NSSO data

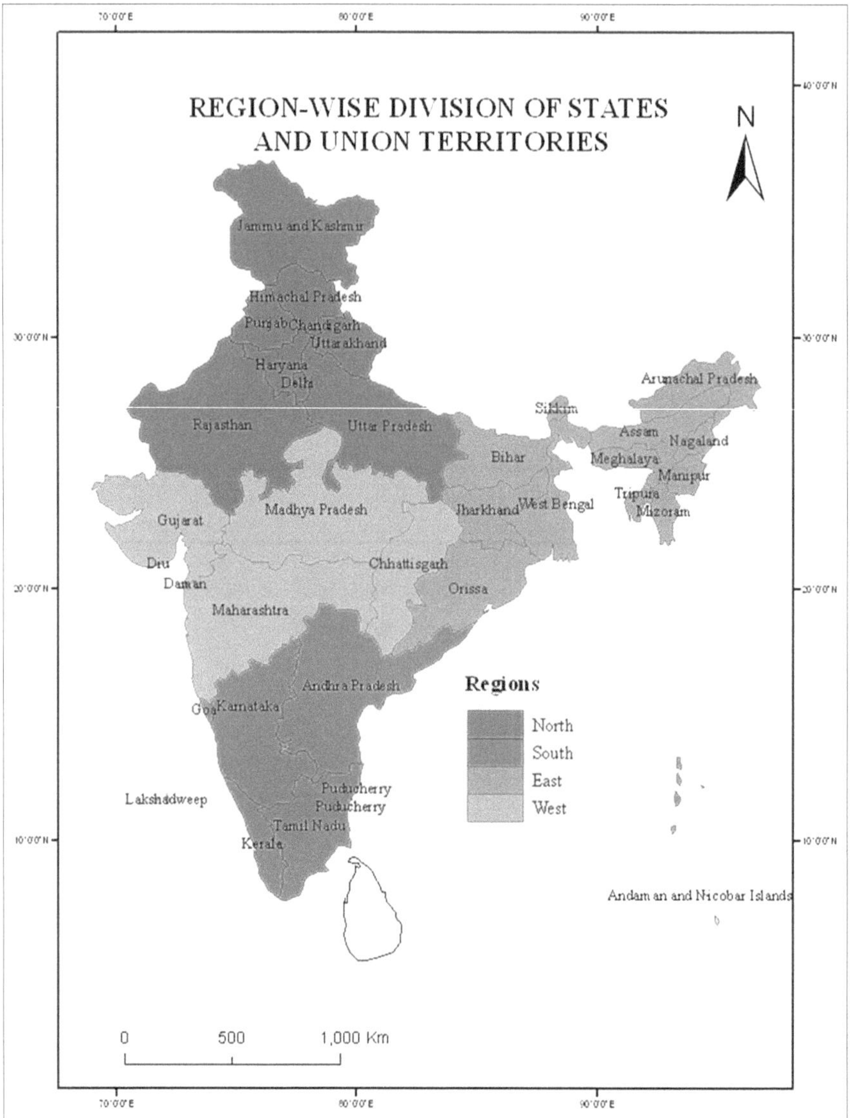

Fig. 5.1 Division of states and UTs of India into different regions

centered on these two types of enterprises. From these two charts we see that the distribution is almost same for the two types of enterprises in south and north region. Only the share of east and west region differs to some extent in the two types of enterprises.

Table 5.3 Region-wise division of states and UTs

Region	State/UT
North	Jammu and Kashmir, Himachal Pradesh, Punjab, Chandigarh, Uttaranchal, Haryana, Delhi, Rajasthan, Uttar Pradesh.
East	Bihar, Sikkim, Arunachal Pradesh, Nagaland, Manipur, Mizoram, Tripura, Meghalaya, Assam, West Bengal, Jharkhand, Orissa.
West	Chhattisgarh, Madhya Pradesh, Gujarat, Daman & Diu, Dadra & Nagar Haveli, Maharashtra.
South	Andhra Pradesh, Karnataka, Goa, Lakshadweep, Kerala, Tamil Nadu, Pondicherry, Andaman & Nicobar Islands.

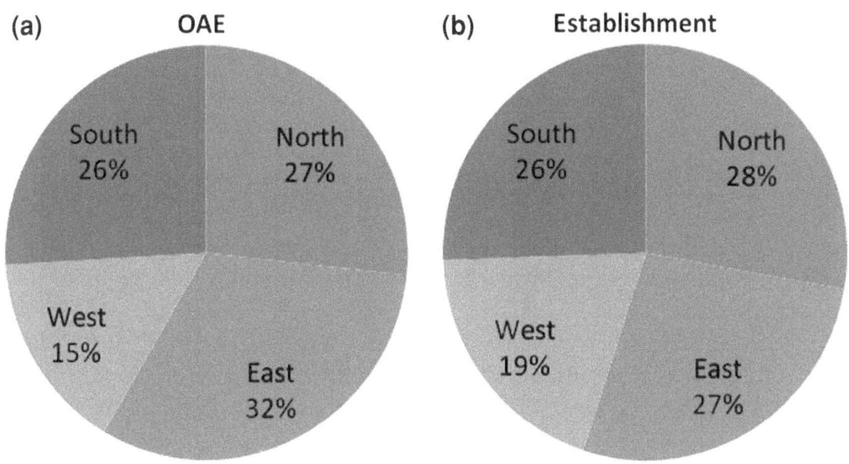

Fig. 5.2 **a** Distribution of OAE enterprises among different regions. **b** Distribution of establishment enterprises among different regions. *Source* Author's own calculations from NSSO data

5.3.4 Average Number of Workers

The labour intensity, measured in terms of the number of workers per enterprise in given in Table 5.4 for each type of enterprise. The difference between the two types of enterprises in terms of labour intensity is substantial. On an average 1.38 persons in OAE and 5.35 persons in establishment were engaged in the service sector. If we compare the different zones in terms of labour intensity in the two types of enterprises, we see that in OAE there is no major difference. But the difference is more pronounced in establishment.

Table 5.4 Average number of workers per enterprise

	OAE	Establishment
North	1.3	5.2
East	1.3	4.6
West	1.4	6.2
South	1.5	5.5
All India	1.4	5.3

Source Author's own calculations from NSSO data

Table 5.5 Percentage of female workers in different zones

	OAE	Establishment	Combined
North	9.7	21.6	17.3
East	13.4	14.5	14
West	11.7	18.3	15.7
South	25.1	27.4	26.5
All India	15.6	20.8	18.8

Source Author's own calculations from NSSO data

5.3.5 Proportion of Female Workers

Gender differential is an important indicator for studying many of the economic variables. In this survey, employment data by gender was also collected in the two types of enterprises, presented in Table 5.5. Nearly every sixth worker was a female in the service sector (when combined both OAE and establishment). The percentage of female labour is relatively higher in establishment than in OAE. In OAE more than 15 % and in establishment about 21 % workers were female. In OAE this percentage is lowest in northern region and highest in southern zone whereas in establishment this figure is lowest in eastern zone and highest in southern zone again. So in the southern zone the participation of women in the unorganised service sector is relatively higher (every fourth worker is a female).

5.3.6 Annual Average Gross Value Added Per Worker and Value of Fixed Asset (in Rs.)

Generally, the relative position of an entrepreneur is determined by the employment size and the value added. In Fig. 5.3 the average gross value added per worker (GVAPW) is given in two types (OAE and establishment) of enterprises in different regions of the country. The annual contribution of a worker in terms of gross value added in this sector was, on an average above Rs. 31,000. It may be seen that there is a significant variation in GVAPW across the two types of enterprises. In all regions, the GVAPW for the enterprise belonging to OAE was lower than those in the establishments. On an average, the value added by a worker in establishment was almost 1.5 times that by a worker in OAE.

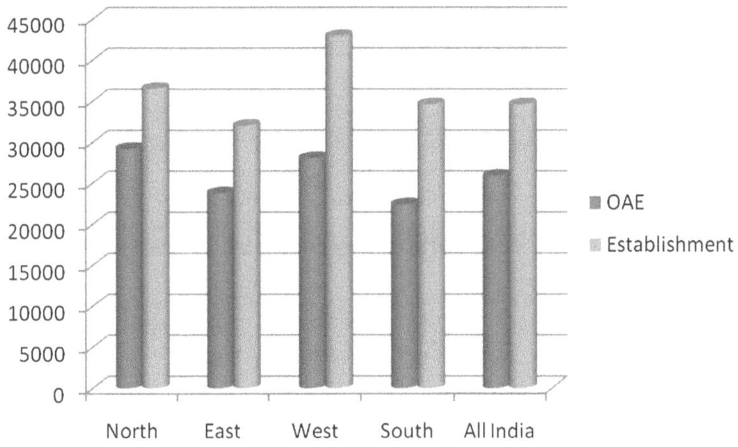

Fig. 5.3 Annual average gross value added per worker (in Rs.). *Source* Author's own calculations from NSSO data

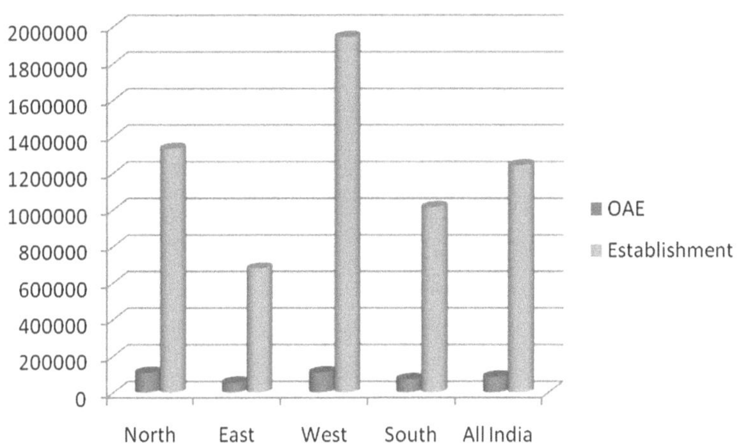

Fig. 5.4 Market value of fixed assets per enterprise (in Rs.). *Source* Author's own calculations from NSSO data

5.3.7 Market Value of Fixed Assets Per Enterprise (in Rs.)

The market value of fixed assets (either owned or hired) held by an enterprise for the purpose of producing goods or services are presented in Fig. 5.4 across different regions. The average value of fixed assets was Rs. 87,731 in OAE and Rs. 1,241,764 in the establishment which indicates that average value of fixed assets in establishments is more than 14 times than that of OAE. The value of fixed assets possessed by an enterprise varied considerably over different regions of the country in both types of enterprises. Among the different zones, west zone has a higher value of fixed assets in both OAE and establishment.

Next we consider some background information about the nature of operation of the enterprises in the service sector.

5.3.8 Distribution of Enterprises by Account Maintenance

From Table 5.6 we see that a very small portion of enterprises in OAE maintains their account. This is true for both regional and all-India level. However in establishment a relatively greater proportion of enterprises maintain account. Within establishment western region ranks first in terms of account maintenance which is well above the all-India average.

5.3.9 Enterprises that Work on Contract Basis

The enterprises in the unorganised sector tend to be small unit. In many cases they are likely to work on a contractual basis under the big units. But our data show that a small percentage of enterprises work on contract basis (Table 5.7).

Table 5.6 Whether account maintained

	OAE		Establishment	
	Yes	No	Yes	No
North	1.51	98.49	8.49	91.51
East	2.55	97.45	12.43	87.57
West	2.09	97.91	15.37	84.63
South	1.11	98.89	8.57	91.43
All India	1.83	98.17	10.92	89.08

Figures represent percentage of total enterprises. *Source* Author's own calculations from NSSO data

Table 5.7 Whether work on contract

	OAE		Establishment	
	Yes	No	Yes	No
North	1.41	98.59	2.20	97.80
East	3.84	96.16	6.85	93.15
West	2.25	97.75	3.93	96.07
South	1.36	98.64	3.22	96.78
All India	2.30	97.70	4.06	95.94

Figures represent percentage of total enterprises. *Source* Author's own calculations from NSSO data

Though the percentage is higher in establishment as compared to OAE, the difference is not so pronounced. This is indicative of independent operation in majority of surveyed cases.

5.3.10 Status of Enterprise Over the Last 3 years

By the status of enterprise, the respondent's impression about the growth or decline of the enterprise in the recent period has been examined. Four possibilities are considered: expanded, stagnant, shrunk and operated less than 3 years. Percentage of enterprises falling under different category is given in Table 5.8. A high percentage of respondents thought that their enterprises have stagnated over the last 3 years, both in OAE and establishment, though the percentage is lower in establishment than in OAE. Next higher category thought that their enterprises have expanded. The feature has remained more or less same in different regions of the country.

5.3.11 Nature of Operation

The seasonality in operations of the enterprise is examined under three heads: Perennial, seasonal and occasional.[1] Almost all the enterprises are run on perennial basis in both types of enterprises (Table 5.9). A negligible portion operates on seasonal and occasional basis.

Table 5.8 Status of enterprise

	OAE				Establishment			
	1	2	3	4	1	2	3	4
North	15.3	46.5	15	23.2	25.2	40	14.3	20.5
East	24.4	57.4	8.4	9.8	35.5	43.4	9.1	12
West	15.1	50.9	14.5	19.5	26.2	42	13.6	18.2
South	13.8	51.5	12.2	22.5	22.9	40.2	11.9	25
All India	17.7	52	12.1	18.2	27.1	41.4	12.2	18.9

1 Expanded, *2* stagnant, *3* shrunk, *4* operated less than 3 years. Figures represent percentage of total enterprises. *Source* Author's own calculations from NSSO data

[1] An enterprise is perennial if the enterprise operates more or less regularly throughout the year. If the enterprise operates during particular season(s) of the year, it is termed as a seasonal enterprise. If the enterprise carries on its activity only occasionally, but total number of days operated in the last 365 days is 30 days or more then it will be treated as a casual enterprise.

Table 5.9 Nature of operation

	OAE			Establishment		
	Perennial	Seasonal	Occasional	Perennial	Seasonal	Occasional
North	98.56	0.96	0.48	98.86	1.02	0.13
East	98.3	1.01	0.69	98.99	0.90	0.11
West	98.74	1	0.26	98.72	1.21	0.07
South	99.34	0.49	0.17	99.37	0.57	0.06
All India	98.71	0.86	0.43	99	0.91	0.10

Figures represent percentage of total enterprises. *Source* Author's own calculations from NSSO data

Table 5.10 Social group of owner

	OAE				Establishment			
	ST	SC	OBC	Others	ST	SC	OBC	Others
North	0.89	14.92	36.11	48.08	0.68	4.11	21.87	73.34
East	6.57	17.64	28.59	47.20	8.73	6.28	24.44	60.54
West	2.57	7.60	37.25	52.59	1.31	3.07	21.02	74.59
South	1.12	7.30	61.97	29.61	0.39	2.54	51.55	45.52
All India	3.02	12.68	40.58	43.73	2.98	4.12	29.97	62.93

Figures represent percentage of total enterprises. *Source* Author's own calculations from NSSO data

5.3.12 Social Group of Owner

From Table 5.10 we see that majority of the owner of the enterprises in both OAE and establishment belongs to the other community (general category). However, in establishment the percentage is greater than that in OAE. The next dominating category is other backward class (OBC). In case of OBC, the percentage is higher for OAE than that in establishment. Then follows the other two categories: SC and ST. Among the different regions, eastern region has a higher percentage of enterprises belonging to the backward classes as compared to other regions.

5.3.13 Type of Ownership

For a majority of the enterprises, the owner is male for both types of enterprises (Table 5.11). However the percentage is lower in case of OAE enterprises. On an average 7–9 % enterprises are owned by female. Only in the southern zone in OAE almost 12 % enterprises are owned by females. In establishment a considerable proportion of enterprises belong to partnership and others.

Table 5.11 Owner of the enterprises

	OAE				Establishment			
	Male	Female	Partnership	Others	Male	Female	Partnership	Others
North	91.91	6.21	1.7	0.19	80.77	6.87	6.8	5.56
East	90.78	7.86	1.05	0.32	85.88	6.57	4.41	3.14
West	89.14	9.26	1.37	0.24	76.52	7.46	8.17	7.85
South	86.05	11.97	1.74	0.24	77.55	7.39	9.15	5.91
All India	89.60	8.70	1.45	0.24	80.51	7.03	7.01	5.43

Figures represent percentage of total enterprises. Partnership means partnership with the members of the same family or from other family; others include co-operative society, limited company and others. *Source* Author's own calculations from NSSO data

Table 5.12 Different types of problems faced by the enterprises

	OAE					Establishment				
	1	2	3	4	5	1	2	3	4	5
North	37.83	0.20	25.82	2.28	33.86	28.98	0.66	31.89	0.24	36.11
East	45.34	0.14	25.15	1.51	27.86	46.41	1.13	27.42	0.18	23.20
West	31.02	0.15	36.13	2.28	30.42	33.96	0.92	35.58	0.21	27.47
South	23.03	0.29	33.06	2.69	40.93	20.84	1.06	35.22	0.28	40.07
All India	35.32	0.20	29.09	2.14	33.25	33.30	0.94	32.78	0.23	30.70

1 Resource constraint, *2* labour problem, *3* social problem, *4* others, *5* no problem. *Source* Author's own calculations from NSSO data

5.3.14 Nature of Problem Faced

Different types of problem faced by the unorganised enterprises are shown in Table 5.12. To simplify presentation, we have aggregated them in some groups.[2] Among the different problems, two major problems faced by the two types of enterprises are resource constraints and social problems. In OAE the main problem is shortage of capital (included in resource). They frequently face difficulties in raising external fund because they rarely have tangible financial security to build in. Another major problem faced by OAE is competition from big enterprises (included in social problem). This is quite a common problem in the era of globalization. In establishments also the main problem is competition from other units.

[2] Within **resource constraint** we include non-availability of electricity, power cut, capital shortage, marketing of product/services, lack of other infrastructure facilities, non-availability of fuel, non-recovery of service charge/fees/credit, **labour problem** includes non-availability of labour and labour unrest, **social problem** includes local problem, harassment and competition from other units, **others** includes problems that are not mentioned above.

Table 5.13 Type of assistance received

	OAE					Establishment				
	1	2	3	4	5	1	2	3	4	5
North	4.4	0.2	0.1	92.8	2.5	9.5	0.2	0.2	87.2	2.9
East	2.7	0.2	0.2	91.8	5.6	8	0.2	0.2	85.1	6.5
West	9.4	0.3	0.1	85.4	4.8	17	0.3	0.1	77.2	5.3
South	15	1.1	0.1	80.6	3.2	24.8	0.3	0.1	70.8	4.1
All India	*19.5*	*1.2*	*0.3*	*76.5*	*2.5*	*14.5*	*0.2*	*0.1*	*80.5*	*4.6*

1 Financial (loan and subsidy), *2* procurement of machinery and raw materials, *3* training and marketing, *4* others, *5* no assistance. All figures represent percentage of total enterprises. *Source* Author's own calculations from NSSO data

Capital shortage is not as critical as OAE. Interestingly, a large percentage of firms report no specific problem. Labour problem is not a vital problem, given the small average number of workers employed in the two types of enterprises (given in Table 4.4).

5.3.15 Type of Assistance Received During the Last Five Years

The enterprises might have received some assistance from government or from some non-government organisation or some private agency/individual. We have grouped them into five categories. Most of the enterprises received different kinds of assistance (mentioned as others) other than financial, procurement of raw materials and training. One-fifth of total enterprises in OAE and establishment received financial assistance. Among the different regions, a greater percentage of enterprises in the southern region got financial assistance from government and other sources. A small percentage of firms (less than 5 %) got no assistance (Table 5.13).

Chapter 6
Gender and Partial Separability: The Indian Experience

6.1 Preliminary Data Analysis

Before we venture into the empirical exercise, it may be pertinent to consider some statistical aspects of the variables used in our models. First we look at some simple statistical properties. These are shown in Table 6.1. Here all variables are expressed in average state-level figures.

The mean value of gross value added is higher in Establishment. But the average employment size is larger in household enterprises (*OAE*) than that in the Establishments. Again the mean value of real Gross Fixed Capital Stock (*GFCS*) is higher in the Establishments than that in *OAE*. This shows that establishment enterprises are more capital intensive than *OAEs*. This is quite expected given that *OAEs* are largely family labour based firms.

However the proportion of women labour to total labour is higher in Establishment than that in the *OAE*s. The situation is contrary to the common belief. It is usually conjectured that due to social restrictions women seldom hire themselves out while they may be employed in the family business to a greater extent.[1] The observed situation can be easily explained by the argument that increased market opportunities open up new vistas for women by commercializing a number of traditional activities.

Next we have considered a few factors which play a significant role on labour productivity.[2] These are given in Table 6.2. Our results indicate that capital intensity played a significant positive role on labour productivity in both types of enterprises. The most interesting finding is that the coefficient of the proportion of female to total worker is significantly negative in OAE and significantly positive in

[1] It can be genuinely argued that the difference between these two proportions is statistically insignificant. However even then the puzzle remains. Women in traditional society are believed to have comparative advantage in home based activities than their male counterpart.

[2] Infact we are trying to estimate the Eq. (4.6) derived earlier. Two types of regressions—linear and log-linear are used in our analysis.

A. Sengupta et al., *Productivity, Separability and Deprivation*, SpringerBriefs in Economics, DOI: 10.1007/978-81-322-1056-6_6,

Table 6.1 Some statistical aspects of the variables

Variables	OAE			Establishment		
	Mean	S.D	C.V	Mean	S.D	C.V
Gross Value Added	8,783.69	11,233.93	127.89	12,582.46	17,402.32	138.3
L_m	3,046,928.64	4,279,012.88	140.43	1,955,868.08	2,398,110.72	122.6
L_f	572,961.6	992,306.80	173.19	494,360	666,196	134.7
L	3,619,890.48	5,087,779.28	140.55	2,449,988.32	3,009,680.96	122.8
λ	0.172	0.1166	0.6783	0.1925	0.1070	0.5558
GFCS	222.9	170.18	76.34	638.63	434.41	68

L_m male labour, L_f female labour. *L* total labour. λ proportion of female to total Labour. *GFCS* gross fixed capital stock. *Source* Author's own calculations from NSSO data

Table 6.2 Sources of productivity variation (dependent variable = labour productivity = y/L)

Independent variable	OAE		Establishment	
	Linear	Log-linear	Linear	Log-linear
Constant	23.458	2.4458	22.852	3.4718
	(9.414)	(12.25)	(3.802)	(23.99)
K/L	0.028564	0.073964	0.0085258	0.053248
	(1.693)	(3.804)	(0.6643)	(2.668)
L_f/L	−11.597	−0.24998	37.342	0.12018
	(1.234)	(−3.514)	(1.917)	(2.143)
D_1	−0.25213	0.0012136	0.22238	0.0050686
	(−2.344)	(0.2331)	(1.074)	(1.194)
D_2	6.5497	0.31063	9.1109	0.23084
	(3.049)	(2.869)	(2.244)	(2.677)
R^2	0.2110	0.3203	0.1014	0.2251

Notes *K/L* capital intensity, D_1 state, D_2 type, L_f/L proportion of female to total labour
Figures in the parentheses represent *t*-values
D_1 and D_2 are the state dummy and locational dummy (rural/urban) respectively

Establishment. This might indirectly hint at a greater productivity of female labour in Establishment than in OAE. The findings seem to support the extended Becker's hypothesis regarding male female dichotomy in work effort that incorporates the effect of increased commercialization.

Finally, we have examined whether Cobb-Douglas production fits well into the data set we used[3] (Table 6.3). The values of R^2 in both types (*OAE* and Establishment) of enterprises suggest that Cobb-Douglas production is compatible with the existing data set. Moreover the corresponding coefficients of capital and labour are highly sig-

[3] We preferred the Cobb-Douglas form instead of other flexible functional forms since the coefficients and shadow price derived from it lends itself to easy interpretation. This interpretation of shadow price is useful because we use it for estimation of female participation function.

Table 6.3 Estimation of Cobb-Douglas production function

Variables	OAE	Establishment
Constant	0.080482	−1.2589
	(0.3414)	(−1.865)
Capital	0.33371	0.40267
	(14.09)	(7.427)
Labour	0.97389	0.95399
	(85.98)	(60.10)
R^2	0.9922	0.9838
F	2183.066	1050.161
Observation	70	70

Note Figures in parentheses represent *t*-values

Table 6.4 Test of labor productivity differentials

Parameters	OAE	Establishment
Constant	0.21209	−0.91066
	(0.94213)	(−1.5450)
α	0.31208	0.38277
	(14.771)	(7.9345)
β	0.97106	0.95306
	(83.468)	(60.856)
γ	0.51064	1.0376
	(2.4439)	(2.7977)
$\theta/1-\theta$	1.95832	0.96376
Log Likelihood	−2.716636	−9.344538
Observation	70	70

Notes For coefficients α and β the null hypotheses are $\alpha = 0$ and $\beta = 0$ and for γ the null hypotheses is $\gamma = 1$. α and β are output elasticity of capital and labour respectively
θ represents quality parameter. $\gamma = (1-\theta)/\theta$ = productivity parameter
Figures in the parentheses represent *t*-values

nificant. We next consider the productivity estimation under the alternative assumptions of separability.

6.2 Estimates Using Partial Separability

For partial separability we have applied the non-linear maximum likelihood method in estimating Eq. (4.11). We have estimated the production function separately for OAE and Establishment in order to take into account any possible difference between them. The estimated values along with *t*-values are presented in Table 6.4. From the *t*-values we find that the coefficients of the variables are highly significant in all the cases. Moreover we find that the output elasticity of capital is higher in Establishments as compared to *OAE*. This clearly indicates a better utilization of capital stock in the Establishment enterprises. However the labour elasticity of output is higher for *OAE*. This supports the standard logic that labour is better utilized in the traditional sector. From the value of the coefficient γ in Table 6.4, we can test the labour productivity differential between *OAE* and Establishment. The value of the coefficient is less than 1 in *OAE* and greater than 1 in Establishment. This shows that males are more productive than females in OAE and females are more productive than males in Establishments. Again the value of the parameter γ is statistically significant in both types of enterprises.

This is a significant finding and throws considerable light on the male–female status in the unorganized service sector in India. In the household enterprises (OAE) a women has to conduct several household chores (such as cooking, washing child rearing etc.) besides being a contributor to the family labour force. Males generally do not share equally with women in this context, thus eventually affecting women's productivity. Thus following Becker (1985) a proper evaluation of women's contribution in the household sector must include not only her direct contribution in the production sphere but also her contribution in the reproduction sphere, simply because the latter is essential for sustaining production activity.[4] The beneficial impact of commercialization on female productivity is manifested in case of establishments.

References

Becker G (1985) Human capital, effort and sexual division of labor. J Labor Econ 3(1):33–58

Abdulai A, Regmi PP (2000) Estimating labor supply of farm households under non-separability: empirical evidence from Nepal. Agric Econ 22(3):309–320

[4] However Abdulai and Regmi (2000) have found no significant differences in male–female Productivity by incorporating time allocated for household purposes in their estimation of labour supply functions. This may however reflect an inherent heterogeneity between time allocated for household chores and that allocated for productivity effort. For females, the former may include a greater intensity of effort per unit of time allocated.

Chapter 7
Gender and Perfect Separability: The Indian Experience

7.1 The Indian Experience

Next we consider the full seperability (**JS**) case. The coefficients of the estimated production functions in the **JS** case are provided in Tables 7.1 and 7.2 respectively. The labour and capital coefficients are significant and the R^2 is quite high. The fit is good enough for further analysis. Using the formulae (4.18) for shadow wages, we then calculate them using the estimated equations.

For comparing average male-female shadow wage among different regions of the country, we have divided all the 35 states and union territories of India into four regions- North, East, West and South. There are 9 states in the Northern region, 13 states in the Eastern region, 7 states in the Western region and the Southern region includes 6 states. The estimated shadow wage shows wide variation across categories and cross-sectional units. In Tables 7.3 and 7.4 we present a summary of our findings. It is seen immediately that on an average female shadow wage is substantially higher than male shadow wage for establishment. However the picture is mixed for OAE. Thus the basic result is almost similar under **JS** and **DV** specifications.[1]

There also exists wide region-wise difference. Interestingly the pattern differs widely for OAE and Establishment enterprises. This proves that commercialization has not taken its root uniformly across the regions. For example the Southern region witnesses lowest marginal productivity for both male and female labour under OAE while for Establishment, the corresponding figure is found to be highest for this region.

Next we compare these shadow wages with the observed wages.[2] A preliminary analysis from the NSS data is presented in Table 7.5. It indicates that in all the sectors women are generally paid less than males. Thus the greater productivity of

[1] In fact the support is partial. Under partial separability males are more productive than female in OAEs. For all India average, there is not much difference between male and female labour.

[2] Unfortunately we do not have the data on wage over each cross-sectional unit. This prevented us from testing the equality of marginal product to the observed wages econometrically as done by some authors (Jacoby 1993; Skoufias 1994; Abdulai and Regmi 2000 etc.).

A. Sengupta et al., *Productivity, Separability and Deprivation*, SpringerBriefs in Economics, DOI: 10.1007/978-81-322-1056-6_7,

Table 7.1 Production function estimates (JS) (OAE)

Variable	Estimated coefficient	T-ratio	*P*-value
Constant	3.5451	30.36	0.000
Lma	0.8208	19.61	0.000
Lfm	0.1058	2.447	0.017
D_1	−0.0694	−2.004	0.049
D_2	0.1497	2.126	0.037
Log(K)	0.0734	8.2444	0.000

Dependent variable = Log(Y). $R^2 = 0.99$ $\bar{R}2 = 0.9894$ F = 2,888.158
D_1 State dummy, *D_2* Type (rural/urban) dummy, *Lma* Log (male labour), *Lfm* Log (female labour), *Log (K)* Log capital

Table 7.2 Production function estimates (JS) (EST)

Variable	Estimated coefficient	T-ratio	*P*-value
Constant	3.8215	29.91	0.000
Lma	0.7154	14.00	0.000
Lfm	0.2255	4.669	0.000
D_1	0.0688	1.671	0.100
D_2	0.2244	2.598	0.012
Log(K)	0.0601	22.509	0.000

Dependent variable = Log(Y). $R^2 = 0.9719$ $\bar{R}2 = 0.9701$ $F = 570.757$
D_1 State dummy, *D_2* Type (rural/urban) dummy, *Lma* Log (male labour), *Lfm* Log (female labour), *Log (K)* Log capital

Table 7.3 Average male/female shadow wage (in Rs.) per worker (OAE)

OAE			
Region	ShW_f	ShW_m	No. of sample
North	37.5633	23.98369	18
	(28.74405)	(5.449247)	
East	18.58298	26.55574	26
	(2.140455)	(1.746049)	
West	33.11911	25.24352	14
	(27.10326)	(7.833808)	
South	9.781124	22.03952	12
	(4.929818)	(5.850837)	
All	24.86197	24.8577	70
	(22.34555)	(7.466739)	

Figures in parentheses represent standard deviation
ShW_f, ShW_m Shadow wage of female and male labour respectively

female labour is not adequately rewarded. In short, though women in most of the cases are no less productive than their male counterparts, their average wage remains on lower side. It is an indirect indicator of *gender deprivation* in the service sector.

Table 7.4 Average male/female shadow wage (in Rs.) per worker (EST)

Establishment			
Region	ShW_f	ShW_m	No. of sample
North	41.47188 (18.34527)	32.12865 (7.340436)	18
East	74.4304 (50.20109)	32.40964 (11.5285)	26
West	89.82668 (75.12988)	35.2513 (7.353146)	14
South	92.65104 (168.2411)	37.43637 (7.053158)	12
All	72.15815 (83.40169)	33.76744 (9.150432)	70

Figures in parentheses represent standard deviation
ShW_f, ShW_m Shadow wage of female and male labour respectively

Table 7.5 Average daily wage per lowest paid full-time unskilled hired worker (in Rs.) for each tabulation category/activity

Rural		*Urban*		*All*	
Male	Female	Male	Female	Male	Female
OAE					
33	28	36	29	35	29
Establishment					
39	28	44	35	42	33
All					
39	28	44	35	42	33

Source NSSO

Table 7.6 Determinants of female participation rate (OAE)

Variable	Estimated coefficient	T-ratio	*P*-value
Log (w_f^*)	−0.86949	−15.33	0
Log (w_m^*)	0.85663	12.23	0
Constant	−1.3992	−3.175	0.002

Dependent variable log (p) where p no of female workers/total workers. Instrumental variable estimation. $R^2 = 0.9937$ $\bar{R}^2 = 0.9935$ $N = 70$
w_f^* and w_m^* are shadow wages of female and male labour respectively

Finally we estimate the female participation function. This is derived from the labour supply function (4.16). Our results present a backward bending tendency for female participation both in OAE and Establishment. Higher the female

Table 7.7 Determinants of female participation rate(EST)

Variable	Estimated coefficient	T-ratio	*P*-value
Log (w_f^*)	−0.64489	−2.34	0.022
Log (w_m^*)	0.81603	10.78	0
Constant	−2.7016	−3.061	0.003

Dependent variable log (p) where p no of female workers/total workers. Instrumental variable estimation. $R^2 = 0.9512$ $\bar{R}^2 = 0.9497$ $N = 70$
w_f^* and w_m^* are shadow wages of female and male labour respectively

shadow wage lower is their supply. This lends support to our supposition that female labour participation is a type of *distress supply* rather than any positive indicator of woman empowerment (Tables 7.6 and 7.7).[3]

7.2 Empirics of Shadow Wage Differentials

An important aspect of the gender differential in productivity is to analyse the factors that can explain such differences. The issue is complex and the data is limited. So we have to contend with the limited data set that is available to us. Productivity basically depends on skills. The skill and dexterity of a worker that adds to his or her productivity may be both general as well as specific. A general level of human skill determines the productive capacity and specific skills add to the productivity in a particular sector. In our study we have tried to capture the general skill by the ratio of female to male literacy rate (LR). On the other hand the NSSO data gives a certain percentage of enterprises that employ only female labour (Ofe). This may be an indicator of skill specificity.

Another important factor is the inmigration of labourers. In fact this point has been raised by Mitra (2005). The inflow of migrant labourers puts pressure on the labour market involving over-use and a fall in productivity. For our analysis we have taken ratio of female to male inmigration. In fact we have considered two categories of in-migration that is available from census data—total migration (Tm) and migration for work (Wm).

Another factor included in our analysis is the percentage of female headed enterprises (Fmh). It may be argued that such enterprises provide a cordial atmosphere for female workers that may boost their productivity.

Our results are shown in Tables 7.8 and 7.9. It is clear that relative female productivity is positively dependent on the relative literacy rate for OAE. The relationship is weird for the Establishment (commercial enterprises). In this case there is a negative relationship between relative female productivity and literacy rate. A simple reason may be that the females with higher level of educational skill may move towards

[3] Our result is in line with the findings of Skoufias (1994).

Table 7.8 Factors explaining the male-female productivity differential in OAE. (Estimate: MLE) dependent variable—(female shadow wage/male shadow wage)

	Model A		Model B	
	Coefficient	T-ratio	Coefficient	T-ratio
LR	1.5321	3.4380*	1.3552	2.156**
Fmh	−0.11829	−1.8539$	−0.12719	−8.535*
Ofe	0.040628	0.57750	0.056778	3.033*
Tm	0.099886	0.51201	–	–
Wm	–	–	−3.8672	−5.748*
St	−0.015900	−1.2525	−0.0058265	−1.956**
Type	−0.57826	−1.8633$	−0.65428	−5.817*
Constant	1.2932	3.9569*	1.8964	5.414*
Log likelihood	−100.71830		−183.290	

Note *, **, $ and $$ represent significance at the 1, 5, 10 and 20 % levels respectively
LR Female to male literacy rate, *Fmh* % of female headed enterprise, *Ofe* % of enterprises with only female worker. *Tm* Ratio of female to male total migration, *Wm* Ratio of female to male Work migration, *St* State dummy, *Type* Rural/Urban dummy–denotes not applicable

Table 7.9 Factors explaining the male-female productivity differential in establishment. (Estimate: MLE) dependent variable—(female shadow wage/male shadow wage)

	Model A		Model B	
	Coefficient	T-ratio	Coefficient	T-ratio
LR	−6.8884	−1.799$	−8.0361	−2.254**
Fmh	0.039258	1.178	0.026009	1.120
Ofe	−0.19231	−4.588*	−0.084445	−1.523$$
Tm	−1.1779	−6.980*	–	–
Wm	–	–	−10.093	−4.069*
St	0.078813	4.465*	0.10606	5.025*
Type	−0.50777	−0.7866	0.054185	0.1523
Constant	8.9001	3.584	8.3985	2.777**
Log likelihood	−363.263		−166.8827	

Note: *, **, $ and $$ represent significance at the 1, 5, 10 and 20 % levels respectively
LR Female to male literacy rate, *Fmh* % of female headed enterprise, *Ofe* % of fnterprises with only female worker, *Tm* Ratio of female to male total migration, *Wm* Ratio of female to male work migration, *St* State dummy, *Type*-Rural/Urban dummy–denotes not applicable

the organized formal sector rather than indulging into informal service activity. It may be noted that Mitra (2005) found a similar negative association with education for the occupational choice model of women workers. So far as specific skill is concerned (Ofe), for OAE there is no significant relation under Model A but positive in Model B. For Establishment the relationship is negative implying that increasing commercialization raises mobility of the female workforce allowing them to compete with their male counterparts. Migration has no effect on the traditional enterprises in Model A. However in Model B this relationship is strictly negative. This implies a negative impact of in-migration on relative female shadow wage through employment of excess labour. Also for the commercial enterprises the relationship is negative. The female entrepreneurship (Fmh) factor has a negative role in the traditional enterprises but the relationship is insignificant in the modern commercial Establishments. Thus the female entrepreneurs have failed to register positive contribution in the informal service sectors. This is a sad story of female entrepreneurship in the informal service sector. However this analysis cannot do proper justice to this very important issue as its focus is different.

The categorical variables such as the state dummy (St) and rural-urban origin (Type) is significant in some of the cases. In short the male-female productivity differential is mainly an outcome of the influence of variation in interregional features rather than of some general factors.

Reference

Mitra A (2005) Women in the urban informal sector: perpetuation of meagre earnings. Devel Change 36:291–316

Skoufias E (1994) Using shadow wages to estimate labor supply of agricultural households. Am J Agric Econ 76(2):215–227

Chapter 8
Deprivation and Gender Divide: Some Issues

Gender deprivation in earning has been revealed by using NSSO data in Chaps. 6 and 7. However, the relationship between deprivation and productivity was rather weak. Hence it is necessary to seek into the causes of gender deprivation through a micro econometric analysis of the unit level data. It is clear that these deprivations have no economic logic behind it. There are social factors that are in action. The micro econometric analysis helps us to unravel the inherent tendencies.

In the 57th round, NSSO collected data on roughly 3.61 lakh firms. There are two categories of firms—Own account enterprises (that don't use hired labour) and the establishment (that utilises hired labour). The former firms are akin to the Chayanovian definition of family firms—that are dependent solely on family labour. The latter category firms are more commercially managed in the use of labour input.

An analysis of these two types of firms is conducted with the sole aim of deciphering their use of female labour—both full time and part time. This is so because it is on this use pattern that the deprivation in earning might be located.

The chapter is divided into three sections. Section 8.1 gives a preliminary analysis of pattern of use of female labour in both of these enterprises. The simple tabular analysis acts as a search light with which we can focus on the origin of women deprivation in earning. Section 8.2 gives the micro econometric limited dependent variable analysis of the phenomena. Section 8.3 tries to fix the ideas revealed from the empirical analysis into a neat diagram.

8.1 Pattern of Female Labour Use: Some Preliminary Features

In order to facilitate our analysis, we have considered three different variables—total fixed asset per worker, percentage of female full time labour and percentage of male full time labour. The first variable gives us an idea of the capital labour ratio. This is an indirect indicator of the enterprise's utilization of technology. NSSO divides total

A. Sengupta et al., *Productivity, Separability and Deprivation*, SpringerBriefs in Economics, DOI: 10.1007/978-81-322-1056-6_8,

workers into full and part time workers. Full time workers are those who work for more than half of the period of normal working hours of the enterprise on a fairly regular basis. On the other hand, persons working for less than or equal to half of the normal working hours of the enterprise on a fairly regular basis have been considered as part time workers. We consider the percentage of female and male full time workers. The full time workers are assumed to give more effort than the part time workers as they work for a longer stretch of time. Hence they should earn more per worker than the part time workers. We segregated the firms first into OAE and Establishment. The variation in full time and part time workers is then notified.

First we have considered three categories of firms—male only, female only and mixed category firms. Male only firms are those which employ only male labours with no female labours. Female only firms are those where only female labours are employed and there is no male labour and mixed firms are those which employ both male and female labour. The proportion of female full time workers is abysmally low when we consider all the firms together. This is true both for OAE and establishment. While under OAE only 10 % of female workers are full time, this is roughly 12 % under establishment. In contrast the male full time is 85 and 86 % respectively (Table 8.1).

The breakup shows the female full time workers are much higher in the female only firms than in the mixed firms. However the number of female-only-firms is itself very low. It is 7 % in OAE and 3 % in establishment. In all, the first category shows that the female composed a very negligible portion of the full time workers.

We now come to the status of enterprises. It captures the respondent's impression about the growth and decline of the enterprise in the recent period. We divide the firms into two categories—expanding and others. Expanding firms are those whose activities are increasing day by day. Within others there are firms which have shrunk, remained stagnant and operated less than three years.

Table 8.1 Distribution of workers according to labour use

	OAE				Establishment			
	Total	Uses male labour only	Uses female labour only	Mixed	Total	Uses male labour only	Uses female labour only	Mixed
Total fixed asset per worker	64,675	68,820	68,201	33,032	144,110	134,550	127,800	176,150
% of female fulltime labour	9.76	–	78.36	37.38	12.03	–	92.97	39.28
% of male fulltime labour	84.7	95.6	–	58.8	86.35	98.74	–	58.69
Total observation	251,488	205,078	175,85	28,825	110,288	81,060	3330	25,898
% of total	100	81.55	6.99	11.46	100	73.50	3.02	23.48

Source Author's own calculations from NSSO data

From Table 8.2 we see that female fulltime workers are much lower in the expanding category of OAE, but are higher in establishment as compared to other category. Again the proportion of expanding firms is significantly lower than the other firms. On the other hand, male fulltime workers are much higher than the female fulltime workers in both categories of firms. So this table also indicates lower fulltime female labour in two types of firms.

Next we consider the distribution of male and female fulltime workers in different enterprises owned by different social groups (Table 8.3). We divide social ownership in two categories—Dalits and General. The Dalit category includes scheduled tribe, scheduled caste and other backward classes. Here again women fulltime workers are significantly smaller in size than the male fulltime workers in all categories.

Consider now the nature of operation, given in Table 8.4. It records the seasonality in operations of the enterprise under survey. There are three types of enterprises in this category—perennial, seasonal and casual. If the enterprise operates more or less regularly throughout the year, it is a perennial enterprise. Seasonal enterprises are those which operate during particular season(s) of the year. On the other hand if the enterprise carries on its activity only occasionally, but total number of days operated in the last 365 days is 30 days or more then it will be treated

Table 8.2 Distribution of workers according to the status of enterprise

	OAE			Establishment		
	Total	Expanding	Non-expanding	Total	Expanding	Non-expanding
Total Fixed asset per worker	64,675	70,839	222,320	144,110	150,560	141,620
% of female fulltime labour	9.76	9.36	26.65	12.03	14.87	10.93
% of male fulltime labour	84.7	86.15	33.76	86.35	83.89	87.3
Total observation	251,488	44,656	206,832	110,288	30,779	79,509
% of total	100	17.76	82.24	100	27.91	72.09

Source Author's own calculations from NSSO data

Table 8.3 Distribution of workers according to the social group of ownership

	OAE			Establishment		
	Total	Dalit	General	Total	Dalit	General
Total fixed asset per worker	64,675	45,255	296,850	144,110	92,610	171,990
% of female fulltime labour	9.76	10.45	8.87	12.03	10.7	12.75
% of male fulltime labour	84.7	84.69	84.71	86.35	87.88	85.52
Total observation	251,488	141,348	110,140	110,288	38,735	71,553
% of total	100	56.20	43.80	100	35.12	64.88

Source Author's own calculations from NSSO data

as a casual enterprise. We see that female fulltime employment is significantly lower than the male fulltime employment in all categories of firms.

Next we consider the firms on the basis of their ownership pattern. We consider two types of firms—those which are owned by females and those owned by others. 'Other' category includes firms owned by male, partnership with the members of the same family or with other family, co-operative society, limited company etc. Here we see that female fulltime employment is comparatively much higher in female owned firms than the other category firms. On the other hand male full time employment is higher in other category firms. This may be due to the fact that females feel much comfort to work in female headed firms than the other category firms. But this does not enhance the women empowerment as the percentage of female owned firms is very low compared to other type of firms (Table 8.5).

Lastly we consider the firms on the basis of their account maintenance activities. There are two types of firms—some firms maintain usable books of accounts and information while others do not. In both types of enterprises proportion of women fulltime employment is considerably lower than the male fulltime employment. Women fulltime employment is higher in commercial firms than the traditional firms (Table 8.6).

Table 8.4 Distribution of workers according to the nature of operation of the enterprises

	OAE			Establishment		
	Total	Perennial	Non-perennial	Total	Perennial	Non-perennial
Total Fixed asset per worker	64,675	64,876	49,326	144,110	144,580	97,628
% of female fulltime labour	9.76	9.81	6.08	12.03	12.11	4.19
% of male fulltime labour	84.7	84.93	67.17	86.35	86.3	91.01
Total observation	251,488	248,242	3,246	110,288	109,182	1,106
% of total	100	98.71	1.29	100	98.99	1.01

Source Author's own calculations from NSSO data

Table 8.5 Distribution of workers according to type of ownership

	OAE			Establishment		
	Total	Other type of ownership	Female headed firms	Total	Other type of ownership	Female headed firms
Total fixed asset per worker	64,675	64,353	68,056	144,110	143,980	402,000
% of female full-time labour	9.76	4.28	67.28	12.03	8.95	52.69
% of male full-time labour	84.7	91.3	15.43	86.35	89.55	44.02
Total observation	251,488	229,605	21,883	110,288	102,530	7,758
% of total	100	91.30	8.70	100	92.97	7.03

Source Author's own calculations from NSSO data

Table 8.6 Distribution of workers according to account maintenance

	OAE			Establishment		
	Total	Maintain	Not maintain	Total	Maintain	Not maintain
Total fixed asset per worker	64,675	186,570	190,960	144,110	272,700	498,400
% of female full-time labour	9.76	10.41	9.75	12.03	18.78	11.2
% of male fulltime labour	84.7	85.44	84.68	86.35	79.59	87.18
Total observation	251,488	4,607	246,881	110,288	12,044	98,244
% of total	100	1.83	98.17	100	10.92	89.08

Source Author's own calculations from NSSO data

The above tabular analysis clearly reveals that the female workforce is not employed mostly as a full time worker. This is true irrespective of the features of the enterprise. The only exception is the 'female only firms'. This is obvious since these firms employ only female labour. However the female-only-firms are a tiny magnitude of the total firms. At least, in percentile terms the male full time workers outweigh the female full time workers.

The reason for non-participation of female workers is sociological. Unfortunately the current NSSO data do not provide us enough information of the workers' personal features. This is a serious drawback of the analysis. Nonetheless it is apparent that social norms and customs make the full time participation of female workers a difficult thing to achieve. The differences in earnings might then be a simple reflection of the social constraints. To fix the idea, a rigorous analysis is required.

8.2 Micro Econometrics of Female Labour Use

Women deprivation has to be indexed by some indicators that are quantitative in nature. There may be several indicators of women deprivation that are utilized in the standard literature (such as gender ratio, gender gap in literacy, gender gap in life expectancy and so on). However, these indicators are not very appropriate for the present study. This is because the study deals with the deprivation of the female workers at their workplace. Hence the employment bias is an important element of deprivation. This bias is not however reflected in the standard deprivation indicators.

There are two aspects of employment bias that might be revealed in the NSSO unit level data. One of the biases is the number of female full time workers as a proportion of total workers (BFT1).

$$\text{BFT1} = \text{Number of full time female workers/Number of total workers} \quad (8.1)$$

In the NSSO data the workers are of three types—full time, part time and exchange workers. The full time workers enjoy a more secure position in the enterprise than the other two types of workers. Hence the proportion of full time workers is an indicator of worker empowerment. Our chosen variable BFT1 measures women empowerment in the context of an enterprise. This indicator will lie between 0 and 1. Larger the value of BFT1, greater is the women empowerment in terms of employment.

Another bias used by us is the distribution of full time workers among male and female. This is measured by the proportion of female full time workers to the total full time workers (BFT2).

$$\text{BFT2} = \text{Number of full time female workers/Number of full time workers} \quad (8.2)$$

This variable measures the extent of female representation among the empowered workers. It is in a way, an estimate of the female share in workers' empowerment. It is a different measure than BFT1. While BFT1 gives the intensity of female empowerment, BFT2 gives us the share of female empowerment. Again it lies between 0 and 1 where a higher value signifies a greater share.

We use a number of explanatory variables in this analysis. The variables above may be categorised into three dimensions—economic variables, social variables and structural parameters. By economic variables we mean those variables which impact on the economic decision making process of the firm. They are important in the day to day activity of the firm and its long run viability. It measures the technique used, managerial and financial decisions. In the following list four variables are of this type (VFAW, SE, NOO and AMC). The social variables are three in number (SGO, TOC and D_1). These variables capture the noneconomic aspects of an individual firm. These variables provide the basic social environment in which the firms operate. Though they are not economic in nature they have important impact on the economic decision making process. Lastly we consider the structural variables (SR and D_2). The structural variables give the locale of the firm. They are more or less historically determined. However their impact on the decision making process of the firm cannot be ruled away. By considering the economic, social and structural factors we hope to unravel the dimension of women empowerment.

Variables used in our analysis

VFAW: Value of fixed asset per worker.
SE: Status of the enterprise—expanding and others. 1 for expanding 0 for others.
NOO: Nature of operation—perennial and others. 1 for Perennial and 0 for others.
SGO: Social group of owner—dalit and general. 1 for dalit and 0 for others.
TOC: Type of ownership code—female and others. 1 for female and 0 for others.
SR: State dummy.
D_1: Firms that employ only male and female labour only. 1 for female and 0 for male.
D_2: Location dummy. 1 for rural and 0 for urban.
AMC: Account maintained or not. 1 for yes and 0 for no.

Now we consider our results. The BFT1 variable is truncated between 0 and 1. Hence the standard OLS technique proves quite inappropriate for this purpose. So we have to consider the Tobit regression technique to analyse the impact of our factors on the proposed measure of women empowerment in employment (BFT1). The Tobit regression clearly indicates some notable features (Tables 8.7 and 8.8). First, almost all the coefficients are significant at 1 % level.

Peculiarly there is a negative relation between women empowerment and capital intensity of firms. Higher the capital intensity, lower is the proportion of women empowerment. This clearly signifies women fell to capture with men in more capital intensive sectors. One of the reasons may be the low educational attainment of female vis-à-vis their male co-workers.

They are more compatible in the sectors with low capital intensity. This is obviously a serious dilemma in our production structure that ought to be corrected.

However, women empowerment is greater in the expanding enterprises. This may be due to the fact that the female workers who are compelled to work to meet their family demand may shirk away from firms when they are contracting and stagnating. The same logic applies for the perennial firms where the women empowerment is larger than in non-perennial firms. Again the female workers are greater empowered in firms that maintain regular accounts.

Now we come to the social variables. The women empowerment is higher in the firms owned by dalit than those owned by general caste. This may be a general reflection of the dalit community where some elements of matriarchal society is still prevent. Also a large portion of female workforce in the informal sector comes from the dalit community. Naturally in traditional own account enterprises the women empowerment is high for the dalit firms. Now coming to the ownership variable, female empowerment is larger in the female owned firms than in the male ownership firms—an obvious result. But female empowerment is lower in firms employing only female laboures.

The first structural variable is SR. This is significant showing a variation across the cross sectional units. The other structural variable is D_2. It is also significant which implies that women are greater empowered in rural firms than the urban firms.

Table 8.7 Tobit estimation (OAE)-BFT1

Variables	Tobit estimates	T-ratio
VFAW	-0.16941×10^{-6}	−10.246
SE	0.50760×10^{-1}	5.1834
NOO	0.69735	17.985
SGO	0.26569	37.395
TOC	1.0733	78.914
SR	0.23808×10^{-2}	65.105
D_1	−1.4145	−94.774
AMC	0.14894	6.020
D_2	0.95855×10^{-1}	14.010
Constant	−1.3475	−32.365

Log likelihood function = −81,925.990 N = 251,488
Dependent variable: gender bias of full time worker (BFT1) = No. of full time female/no. of workers

Table 8.8 Tobit estimation (establishment)-BFT1

Variables	Tobit estimates	T-ratio
VFAW	0.15336×10^{-7}	2.2576
SE	0.25560	28.706
NOO	0.43523	8.0968
SGO	−0.14867	−16.382
TOC	0.98756	68.447
SR	0.21531×10^{-2}	50.395
D_1	−1.5471	−73.860
AMC	0.42810	36.464
D_2	−0.11533	−12.124
Constant	−0.21065	−3.6052

Log likelihood function = −52,467.465 N = 110,288
Dependent variable: gender bias of full time worker (BFT1) = No. of full time female/No. of workers

We now consider the establishment firms. Here also all the variables are significant at 1 % level. Unlike OAE, in establishment, there is a positive relation between women empowerment and capital intensity of firms. Higher the capital intensity, higher is the women empowerment. This indicates that women can compete with men in more capital intensive sectors. It may be due to the fact that these firms run on commercial basis with hired labour. So they must be more compatibles with higher capital intensive establishment firms in order to sustain in this sector.

Like OAE, women empowerment is greater in the expanding enterprises as well as in perennial firms. The reasons are the same as in OAE. As before the female workers are greater empowered in firms that maintains regular accounts.

Coming to the social variables, we see that women empowerment is lower in the firms owned by dalits as compared to firms owned by general caste. This is due to the lower access to working capital by dalits, as revealed by different studies. Naturally in commercial enterprises, which are more capital intensive, women empowerment is low for the dalit firms. Here also, female empowerment is larger in the female owned firms than in the male owned firms. Female empowerment is also lower in firms employing only female labourers.

Here also the structural variable, SR is significant showing a variation across the cross sectional units. But, the other structural variable, D_2 is negative implying that women empowerment is greater in urban firms than the rural firms.

Next we consider our results for the BFT2 variable which is also truncated between 0 and 1. By the same logic we have considered the Tobit regression technique to analyse the impact of different variables on women empowerment in employment. Almost all the coefficients are significant at 1 % level (Tables 8.9 and 8.10).

Here we get the similar result like BFT1. There is a negative relation between women empowerment and capital intensity of firms. Women empowerment is greater in the expanding enterprises, in the perennial enterprises and in firms that maintain regular accounts.

Table 8.9 Tobit estimation (OAE)-BFT2

Variables	Tobit estimates	T-ratio
VFAW	-0.11547×10^{-6}	−7.0242
SE	0.76237×10^{-1}	8.1222
NOO	1.1780	30.526
SGO	0.31114	40.452
TOC	0.87381	62.854
SR	0.19776×10^{-2}	50.119
D_1	−0.41685	−28.334
AMC	0.16356	6.171
D_2	0.76005×10^{-2}	1.028
Constant	−3.0725	−73.615

Log likelihood function = −453,300.65 N = 251,488
Dependent variable: gender bias of full time worker (BFT2) = No. of full time female/No. of full time workers

Table 8.10 Tobit estimation (establishment)-BFT2

Variables	Tobit estimates	T-ratio
VFAW	0.28319×10^{-7}	4.2331
SE	0.22678	23.838
NOO	0.75887	11.705
SGO	-0.85472×10^{-1}	−8.7556
TOC	0.70986	48.183
SR	0.14218×10^{-2}	31.185
D_1	−0.36994	−18.221
AMC	0.36492	29.573
D_2	−0.13781	−13.383
Constant	−1.9357	−28.186

Log likelihood function = −312,211.94 N = 110,288

Again women empowerment is higher in the firms owned by dalit and in the female owned firms. But female empowerment is lower in firms employing only female laboures.

The SR variable is significant. But the D_2 variable is insignificant, implying no difference between rural and urban enterprises, so far as women empowerment is concerned.

Lastly we consider the establishment firms for the BFT2 variables. All the variables are significant. There is a positive relation between women empowerment and capital intensity of firms. Likewise women empowerment is greater in the expanding and perennial enterprises as well as in firms that maintains regular accounts.

Women empowerment is lower in the firms owned by dalits, in firms employing only female laboures, but is higher in the female owned firms.

The SR variable is significant and D_2 is negative implying that women empowerment is greater in urban firms than the rural firms.

8.3 Explanatory Analysis in the Female Labour Use

Gauging through the mess of data as revealed by the tabular analysis and econometric analyses carried on in this book, we come to a very interesting conclusion. It appears that there are two stylised facts regarding the female labour in India.

Fact 1 Women workers have a higher marginal product than the male workers
Fact 2 In terms of payment per worker, women are paid much less than male

These two facts can be reconciled only if we are ready to introduce the labour-laborer distinction, first introduced by Prof. A. K. Sen (1967). The essence of the argument is simple. Two workers may not put equal amount of effort in conducting a particular job. Thus the amount of labour services that might be expected from a labourer may differ from individual to individual. Unlike the standard economic theory the equivalence between the labour and labourer breaks down. The key concept here is the amount of effort that a labourer puts in when he/she works.

To illustrate this we use a simple diagram. We consider two cases—(1) when both the male and female workers are equally productive i.e. operate on the same marginal product curve (Fig. 8.1) and (2) where for each unit of labour effort,

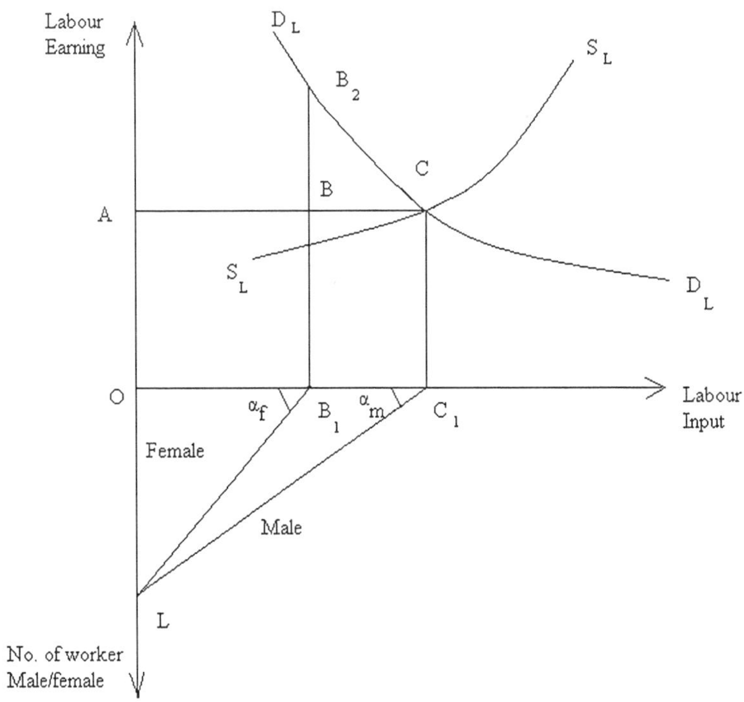

Fig. 8.1 Both male and female workers have the same marginal product curve

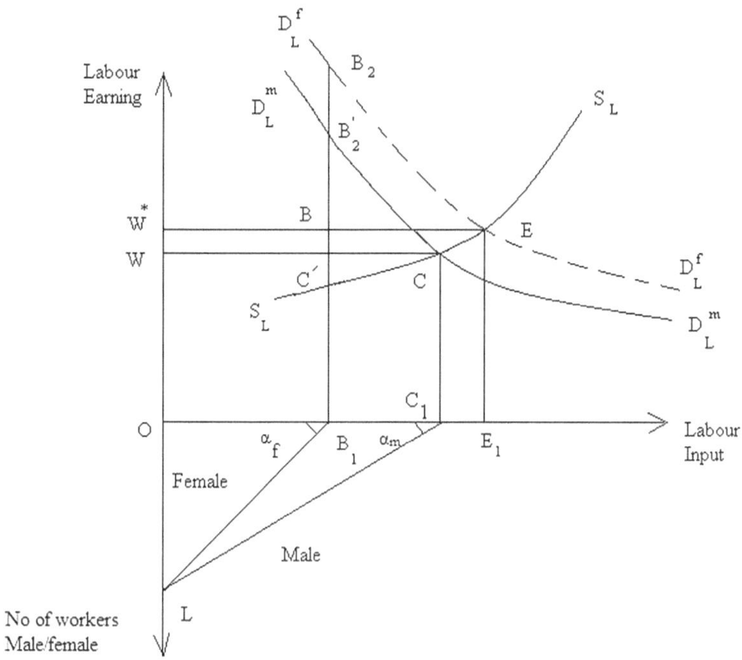

Fig. 8.2 Marginal product curve of female is higher than that of male

females are more productive than males. The marginal product curve of female dominates that of the male (Fig. 8.2).

In Fig. 8.1 there are two diagrams imposed on one another. The 'top' axis from origin O measures labour earning, while the bottom axis measures the number of workers (male/female). D_LD_L is the common marginal product (MP) curve of male and female labour. S_LS_L is the standard upward rising labour supply curve. Now suppose the firm requires OL amount of male and OL amount of female workers.[1] OL male gives effort OC_1 (at the rate α_m) and earns an earning $OACC_1$. However, the OL female provide effort OB_1 ($OB_1 < OC_1$) with rate α_f. The total earning is now $OABB_1$. Since $OABB_1 < OACC_1$, it is easy to see the earning per male is greater than the earning per female. However, the MP of OB_1 female effort is B_1B_2. Obviously this exceeds the male MP, CC_1 by the simple law of diminishing marginal product.

Now, let us assume that the females are more productive than male and they have a diminishing MP curve $D_L{}^f\, D_L{}^f$. In this case again the female earning is OB_1BW^*. By comparison, we find that the common area is $OWC'B_1$. The female area is $WC'BW^*$. The male area is $B_1C'CC_1$. If the female MP curve is not too far away, the male area is greater than the female area. Consequently the male

[1] We are considering the perfect separability case.

earning per worker is larger than the female earning per worker even in this case. However, the MP of the female workers is now B_1B_2 which not only exceeds the male MP (CC_1), but also the female MP in case 1 (B_1B_2').

Thus we see that the lower intensity of female labour effort translate into their lower earning, even though they are technically much more productive than the male co-workers. Since these differences in participation are sociological in nature, the women deprivation in earning has its origin in non-economic roots.

This chapter is a micro-econometric analysis of the firm level data constituting the NSSO reports. The dimensions of women deprivation in employment is directly related to their job security and the nature of their participation. The Indian data shows that there are a number of economic, social and structural factors that determine the length and breadth of women deprivation. Going through all the analysis, we have to conclude that the source of women deprivation is not economic but rather social. Removal of these social barriers is a sure way to end much of the deprivation. Our policy makers should concentrate on the policies to combat social discrimination of females.

Reference

Sen AK (1967) Surplus labour in India: a critique of Schultz's statistical test. Econ J 77 (305) March:154–161

About the Authors

Atanu Sengupta M.Sc., Ph.D from the Indian Statistical Institute, India. He has been teaching as an associate professor at the Department of Economics, Burdwan University, West Bengal, India for the past 10 years. He has supervised 5 M.Phil. theses and 10 Ph.D dissertations. He has published about 45 papers in various refereed national and international journals. He has also published 6 books. His areas of interests are in Econometrics, Financial Economics, Development Economics, Microeconomics and Growth Theory.

Soumyendra Kishore Datta M.A., M.Phil., Ph.D., Post Doctoral study from York University, U.K. is a professor of economics at the Department of Economics, Burdwan University, West Bengal, India. He has been teaching at university level for the last 22 years, has supervised 24 M. Phil. theses and 11 Ph.D. dissertations. He has published more than 45 papers in various reputed national and international journals. He specializes in teaching environmental economics, industrial organization and game theory, microeconomics, statistics etc.

Susanta Mondal M.Sc., Ph.D. He has been teaching at the college level for the last 6 years. He has been actively engaged in research work. He has published 3 papers in reputed journals.

A. Sengupta et al., *Productivity, Separability and Deprivation*,
SpringerBriefs in Economics, DOI: 10.1007/978-81-322-1056-6,

Index

A. Sengupta et al., *Productivity, Separability and Deprivation*,
SpringerBriefs in Economics, DOI: 10.1007/978-81-322-1056-6,

FSC
www.fsc.org
MIX
Papier | Fördert
gute Waldnutzung
FSC® C083411

Kolibri 360 GmbH
Ferdinand-Jühlke-Straße 7
99095 Erfurt, Deutschland
produktsicherheit@kolibri360.de